Praying the Lord's Prayer Today

KENNETH SLACK

Praying the Lord's Prayer Today

SCM PRESS LTD

334 01289 9

First published 1973
by SCM Press Ltd
56 Bloomsbury Street London

© Kenneth Slack 1973

Printed in Great Britain by
Cox & Wyman Ltd
London, Fakenham and Reading

CONTENTS

Contents

The 'Our Father' contains all possible petitions; we cannot conceive of any prayer which is not already contained in it. It is to prayer what Christ is to humanity. It is impossible to say it once through, giving the fullest possible attention to each word, without a change, infinitesimal perhaps but real, taking place in the soul.

Simone Weil, *Waiting on God*

Jesus told his disciples not only *how* to pray, but also what to pray. The Lord's Prayer is not merely the pattern prayer, it is the way Christians *must* pray. If they pray this prayer, God will certainly hear them. The Lord's Prayer is the quintessence of prayer.

Dietrich Bonhoeffer, *The Cost of Discipleship*

INTRODUCTION

This short book originated in three ways. Some years ago I read Gerhard Ebeling's *The Lord's Prayer in Today's World* (SCM Press 1966). I was greatly stimulated by it, yet aware that in many ways the manner in which the great German scholar-preacher handled the Bible remained foreign to the Anglo-Saxon mind. (Bishop F. R. Barry in his autobiography *Period of My Life* (Hodder & Stoughton 1970) refers to the total bewilderment of Nottinghamshire parishioners when confronted by this phenomenon from non-Aryan German refugees who had been ordained to the Anglican ministry). Ebeling's book nevertheless alerted me to the need for the Christian teacher to be constantly relating the Lord's Prayer to today's world, and in one sense this book is an attempt to do that without a merely ephemeral topicality.

One other way in which this book originated was growing awareness of the degree to which modern scholarship had illuminated the prayer. Here I mention especially just a few pages in which, with characteristic simplicity, T. W. Manson reveals this in his *The Sayings of Jesus* (SCM Press 1949, pp. 167ff.). A definitive study of the Lord's Prayer, which is perhaps more of a quarry than a building, will be found in Ernst Lohmeyer's *The Lord's Prayer* (Collins 1965).

This book is not, however, primarily an attempt to bring to the general reader the result of that modern research. I have no equipment for this, and it has been admirably done by Professor

C. F. Evans in his *The Lord's Prayer* (SPCK Seraph Book 1963). It is intended to help the ordinary Christian to pray this prayer with increased understanding and a sense of its relevance to this, as to every, age. For the third way in which this book originates is in the simple request from a member of my church to whom I had given a lift that I would preach a series of sermons on prayer. What better response could there be than to turn to the Lord's Prayer? What now appears is only distantly related to what was said from the pulpit, but the request and the response to my attempt to meet it encouraged me to feel that it was worthwhile to go on working at this theme. One of the fascinations of doing this has been constantly to find that shafts of light on this prayer have come from the most varied general reading across many months. What testimony this is to the universality of this prayer!

Once again I am most indebted to my friend and publisher, John Bowden, for encouragement in the enterprise, and to my friend and secretary, Winifred Weddell, for invaluable help in bringing it to completion.

I

VAIN REPETITIONS

During war-time service in India I walked into Tibet. Then, before the Chinese invasion, it could have been called the most religious country in the world. Its head was the Dalai Lama, believed to be the reincarnation of past holders of that high-priestly office, and all communities were centred upon the Buddhist monasteries. On the high thresholds of that land, the Natu La and Jelep La passes, each some fourteen thousand feet above sea level, there fluttered long lines of tattered prayer flags. Not only the monks in the monasteries but the wayside beggars turned the prayer wheels that held the tightly-wound rolls of prayers and murmured 'Om mani pani sum'. . . .

On the way out from that expedition my eye was caught by an unusual object. It was a great drum below which were paddle-wheels that were being turned by the rush of water from a narrow stream that tore down the Himalayan hillside. The drum turned swiftly, and our guide explained that it, too, was a prayer-wheel, within which were the coils of the written prayers. Even the element of personal demand represented by the turning of the prayer-wheel by that trick of the wrist you have to learn before being able to use one had been removed. Night and day, without human intervention, nature's forces offered men's prayers; the bitter wind sweeping across the high passes or the forceful torrent coming down the hillside animated the prayers and cease-lessly repeated them.

'But when ye pray, use not vain repetitions, as the heathen do.'[1]

Involuntarily the words of Jesus came into my mind. They are words that form part of the setting of Jesus teaching his followers how to pray, giving them, in fact, the Lord's Prayer. Matthew's account of the gift of the prayer sets it within the Sermon on the Mount. Neither conventional reverence towards other people's religion, or a sense of embarrassed shame that they seem so much more religious than we are, should be allowed to blunt the sharpness of Jesus' command. He is decisively breaking his followers away from that whole conception of religion.

One reason for the 'vain repetitions' was that those who used them were polytheists, believing in 'gods many, and lords many',[2] as Paul put it. That meant that in prayer they used the shot-gun technique, peppering the whole wide target with names and epithets and phrases in the hope that one of them would strike a target and gain an answer to their need. For Jesus nothing could be more out of keeping with prayer to the God who had revealed himself. You do not pray in that way to the God who has shown himself to men.

This has something to say to our manner of public prayer today. It is not only our present suspicion of verbalizing that will question the piling up of modes of address to God in the opening of prayers; 'Eternal God, Mighty in power, Omnipotent Ruler over all things in heaven and in earth' – prayers after that fashion. Some justification for this may be sought in the argument that it is a tuning of the spirits of the worshippers, as not a little of public prayer must be. It is inadequate justification, though, for too readily it slides towards vain repetitions, and always it is a departure from that total simplicity of address which Jesus commands, and which he himself used.

When you look at the modern translations of these words of Jesus that introduce his teaching of his prayer to his followers, you find a fresh emphasis emerging. J. B. Phillips' translation reads: 'And when you pray don't rattle off long prayers like the pagans who think they will be heard because they use so many words. Don't be like them.' The New English Bible renders it: 'In your prayers do not go babbling on like the heathen, who imagine that the more they say the more likely they are to be heard. Do not imitate them.' Here the emphasis is not on peppering the target but, (to use another metaphor drawn from armament), laying down such an artillery barrage that no opposition to your desires can survive.

Again, part of the condemnation is surely that such a way of praying shows ignorance of who is being addressed. Anyone who has to write a letter that will be read by a mass of different and only partly-known people knows what an unsatisfactory business it is. (Observe the average letter from vicar or minister in the local church news-sheet for ready examples.) There is all the difference in the world between that and the letter that you write to one person. In the latter case a few words will often serve to convey meaning in a simple and direct way, because you know whom you are addressing. Jesus told us that this must be the mark of Christian prayer.

This is not the whole condemnation of the kind of prayer that could be described as 'rattling off' or 'babbling on'. Another part of it must surely have been its mindlessness. Christians would have done well to take more notice of their Master's injunction to love the Lord their God with all their mind, as well as with heart and soul. This does not mean that there are intellectual qualifications for the life of prayer: it means that we must not abandon what mind we have got when we speak to God. The simplest person uses his mind in the skills of his daily work and in speaking to other people. Jesus tells us to do no differently when we come to speak to the Father.

The final condemnation of such prayer must be that in so far as any character is attributed to God by the use of such a mode of speech to him, it is a wholly lamentable one. I put it with deliberate crudity; to rattle off endless demands like that is to believe that if you were not to keep badgering God he would fall down on the job. We misapply Jesus' parable of the importunate widow and the reluctant judge when we use it as justification for that form of prayer. When Paul bids us pray without ceasing[3] he cannot be referring to our formulated prayers put into words. In that sense life must be more than praying: in another and profounder sense our praying can turn all life into prayer. Our praying, if it be praying guided by the Lord's Prayer, is a turning away from self towards God and that self-disregarding life to which God calls us. A life that has gained its compass-bearing from moments of such prayer could rightly be described as ceaseless prayer. As W. H. Auden has said: 'To pray is to pay attention to something or someone other than oneself. Whenever a man so concentrates his attention – on a landscape, a poem, a geometrical problem, an idol, or the True God – that he completely forgets his own ego and desires, he is praying.' To this striking definition the poet feels bound to add the warning that a man is responsible for the choice of that on which he so concentrates his attention, 'and must accept the consequences'.[4] The man who concentrates his attention on God revealed in Jesus Christ in times of conscious prayer seeks to pray without ceasing by gaining for all his living a concentration on others and on all that is lovely and of good report.

Most of the following pages must of necessity concentrate on particular phrases and details of the Lord's Prayer. It is good before we plunge into this to stand back and mark its character as a whole. When we do this its most remarkable feature is its brevity.

Here is a prayer of which Simone Weil could say it 'contains all possible petitions; we cannot conceive of any prayer which is not already contained in it',[5] but the whole prayer in its most familiar English version (without the later-added ascription at the close) contains only fifty-three words. This short series of almost stark petitions comprehends all that Jesus had to say when (according to Matthew's account) he gave his followers a different way of prayer to be set over against the vain repetitions of the heathen, or (according to Luke's account) he responded to the direct request of those followers that he should teach them to pray.

Pray briefly, mindfully, and pointedly – this seems to be as much part of his teaching about prayer as any of the content of individual phrases.

In fact it is the spareness, the stripped-down quality, of the Lord's Prayer which chiefly gives it an original character. It has been pointed out that most of its phrases can be paralleled in the prayers of Jewish piety at the time of Jesus. T. W. Manson quotes in his *The Sayings of Jesus* an ingenious construction that has been made of a prayer which wholly derives from Jewish sources and contains all that the Lord's prayer contains. It reads:

> Our Father, who art in Heaven. Hallowed be Thine exalted Name in the world which Thou didst create according to Thy will. May Thy Kingdom and Thy lordship come speedily, and be acknowledged by all the world, that Thy Name may be praised in all eternity. May Thy will be done in Heaven, and also on earth give tranquillity of spirit to those that fear thee, yet in all things do what seemeth good to Thee. Let us enjoy the bread daily apportioned to us. Forgive us, our Father, for we have sinned; forgive also all who have done us injury; even as we also forgive all. And lead us not into temptation, but keep us far from all evil. For thine is the greatness and the power and the dominion, the victory and the majesty, yea all in Heaven and on earth. Thine is the Kingdom, and Thou art Lord of all beings for ever. Amen.[6]

How very familiar it seems, yet how padded out, and therefore how different. Dr Manson sees the originality of the Lord's Prayer as lying 'in the composition as a whole, in the choice of just these petitions and no others, in the arrangement of them, in its brevity and completeness'.[7] Jesus ruthlessly pared down the piety of his own upbringing. This was not done in order that prayer might not obtrude on the day's business, for over against the brevity of Jesus' pattern prayer must be set what the gospels record about the leisureliness of his daily conversation with his Father. Rather was it in order that the guidelines might be so simple as to be totally unmistakable. To those guidelines we now turn.

NOTES

1. Matt. 6.7 (AV)
2. I Cor. 8.5 (AV)
3. I Thess. 5.17 (AV)
4. W. H. Auden, *A Certain World*, Faber 1971, p. 306.
5. Simone Weil, *Waiting on God*, Collins Fontana 1959, p. 177.
6. T. W. Manson, *The Sayings of Jesus*, SCM Press 1949, p. 167.
7. Manson, op. cit., p. 168.

2

OUR FATHER

The teaching of Jesus about prayer sprang from his experience in prayer. Even the disciples' demand that he should teach them how to pray, according to Luke, sprang from the impression that they had of Jesus when he prayed. 'Once, in a certain place, Jesus was at prayer. When he ceased, one of his disciples said, "Lord, teach us to pray, as John taught his disciples."'[1] It was not that they did not know how to pray. Every Jewish child was instructed in private prayers to be said daily, and was trained in the public prayer of the synagogue. It is implied, too, that they knew John's way of praying. But there was that in the sight of Jesus praying which suggested that if he were to teach them how to set about it prayer might have a new dimension added to it. What the gospels reveal to us about the prayers of Jesus will prove to be the best commentary that we can have on the Lord's Prayer.

If there was no division between Jesus' practice of prayer and his teaching about it, we can also believe that there was no division between his experience of life and the understanding of prayer to which he came. Modern psychology and sociology have illuminated the tragic inability of those who have had no experience of love to believe that it exists. They speak of the ineradicable damage done to young lives by deprivation of affection. In the light of this it is surely not an over-use of the imagination which sees Christian men owing a greater debt to Joseph the carpenter than the church has traditionally acknowledged. As the poet Andrew Young has put it, '... the Boy grew up with a happy, even holy, experience of his home. The familiar word with which he addressed Joseph, Abba, Dear Father, was the word with which he came to address God.'[2] The same writer roundly affirms that the writer of the fourth gospel was mistaken in setting the words, 'Holy Father' on Jesus' lips in prayer, for the added word 'implied a distance he did not feel'.[3]

Certainly all the gospel evidence is that the word 'Father', alone and unqualified, was Jesus' normal way of speaking to God. The one occasion in the first three gospels on which he is described as crying 'My God' is in the cry of dereliction from the cross, and – whatever we may judge to be the meaning of his using them – these words are part of the twenty-second psalm. When, also from the cross, he draws upon deep memory of the words of praise in his dying moments and uses words from Psalm 31, 'Into thy hands I commend my spirit', he makes them his own by adding the word, 'Father'. George Adam Smith wrote: 'The Gospels give us many of the prayers of Jesus; and I think I am right when I say there is not one which fails to address God as Father.'[4]

These facts alone would give immense force to the teaching of Jesus that his followers were to speak to God with the confidence and simplicity of sons. Every attentive reader of the New Testament must be aware of the significant way in which the early church not only preserved this fact but the actual sound that Jesus made when he said the word himself. That sound was the Aramaic word, 'Abba'. It seems as though the first Christians delighted in forming with their lips the actual word spoken by their Lord when he said this name that was the heart of what he understood by faith. Mark records it of Jesus' prayer in Gethsemane: 'Abba, Father, all things are possible to thee; remove this cup from me; yet not what I will, but what thou wilt.'[5] Paul, writing to the church at Rome and giving his most profoundly thought-out understanding of man's co-operation with God in prayer, says: 'When we cry "Abba! Father!" it is the Spirit himself bearing witness with our spirit that we are the children of

God.'[6] Earlier, writing to the churches of Galatia he said: 'God has sent the Spirit of his Son into our hearts, crying, "Abba! Father!".'[7]

So characteristic of Jesus was this word that even non–Aramaic-speaking disciples seem to have understood and relished the sound. Moreover, scholars have discovered that those early Christians who spoke, or had a knowledge of, Aramaic would have a good reason for remembering this sound, even when the Greek of common-or-garden speech around the Roman empire was their normal means of communication. This had to do with the actual form in which Jesus used the Aramaic word that stood for 'Father'. It is not, as at first glance, it might appear to be, a point only for pedant or grammarian; it sends a shaft of light right home to Jesus' understanding of God himself.

The way in which the word was used was shown by the suffix, that is, how it ended. Where we would say 'my father' or 'his father' or 'your father' an Aramaic-speaker would end the word that began with 'abb-' in one particular way. Ernst Lohmeyer tells us that 'The religious language of Judaism does not, however, know the word *abba*, which is limited to everyday usage; for greater sanctity it prefers the obsolete Hebrew forms.'[8] That phrase about 'everyday usage' gives us one of the clues to the use by Jesus of this form. 'Abba' was the way in which a son addressed his own father. Until Jesus came that was the limitation of the use of the word. Dr Manson puts it like this:

> This way of speaking of one's earthly father does not hold when speaking of the Father in heaven. Jewish piety felt it unfitting to speak of God or to God in the same familiar and intimate way in which one spoke of or to one's earthly father. Therefore when 'my Father' means God the form with the suffix, *abī*, takes the place of the simple *abba*. Jesus abolished this distinction.[9]

It would be difficult to exaggerate the importance of that last sentence, and all it must mean for a recasting of many of our religious conceptions if we have not taken this fact seriously. 'Jesus abolished this distinction.' It means that the word 'Father' when used of God must never for one moment have less intimacy about it (though it may have far more reverence) than when it is applied to a man. It means that we worship not a distant all-powerful being who, from time to time, in his occasional graciousness, condescends to show a fatherly aspect in his dealings with men but one who, through and through, is Father.

Now the use of such a word involves large questions of the use of religious language. Those who would like to follow up this point are referred to the second chapter of Professor C. F. Evans' *The Lord's Prayer*. What in fact do we mean when we call God 'Father'? Professor Evans tells us: 'Some form of address to God or gods as "father" would appear to be as old and widespread as religion, as mankind itself.' Obviously the use of such a word is of the nature of 'picture' language, and no one, since the publication of Bishop John Robinson's *Honest to God*, can have any doubt about the importance of 'images' of this kind in our religious thinking.

Two basic and essential points must be made for our purpose in studying the Lord's Prayer. One is that for Jesus the word 'Father' was not one among many pictures used in thinking of God and speaking to him. It was *the* picture. In the Old Testament the word 'Father' will be found used of God, as in 'Like as a father pitieth his children, so the Lord'[10] (though here, we may note, the stress is on God's fatherly activity rather than his nature as Father). In this usage, however, 'Father' is only one of a number of names for God. Some of them are used far more frequently. As we have seen, Jesus in prayer always addresses God as 'Father' *and never as anything else*.

Nor is it only that Jesus uses the word 'Father' exclusively; as we have seen, he invests it with the fullest possible content. Far from half-apologizing for using so human a picture – as in a sense the psalmist does in his 'Like as a father' – he makes the word as human as it can be. His word for 'Father', 'Abba', is the common workaday word used by a son when he spoke to his father, and one which, for that very reason, had been avoided in religious use before Jesus. By his exclusive use of this word for God, and his use of it in a form which is unmistakable in its plain meaning, Jesus confronts us with a number of challenges.

There is one challenge we cannot escape if we are honestly to pray the Lord's Prayer in today's world. It is whether we *can* pray to God, the ultimate reality of this world, and with integrity address him as 'Father'. At the eucharist, according to the Book of Common Prayer, the words that lead to the people of God saying the Lord's Prayer together are 'we are bold to say'. I suppose that the original meaning was an expression of wonder that we frail creatures can dare to address our maker in this intimate form. Perhaps a secondary meaning that the actual words will support may be stronger for many worshippers today. You arrive in church with the images of last night's television news and the special reports from the world's trouble-spots still flickering in your consciousness. The devastation of a tidal wave or earthquake, the grim pathos of a ward full of children who are napalm victims, reports, with pictures, of some atrocity against a great number of people – all these, and more, give a searing sense of almost universal suffering and of a cosmos which has self-destruction rather than fatherly love as its heart and meaning. With all this in mind and heart the familiar words of the liturgy 'we are bold to say "Our Father"' take on a new meaning. Bold it is, indeed, to claim by such a word that, as I believe, T. R. Glover put it, the heart of the universe is 'more like a father's loving heart than anything else that we know'.

The plain answer is that the Lord's Prayer is a prayer for Christ's men and women. We are only 'bold to say, Our Father' in the face of a world like ours because Jesus has shown us that this is the nature of ultimate reality. Bishop John Robinson in his *The Difference in Being a Christian Today*, when he writes of love being that ultimate reality, says

What evidence is there for such an estimate of the cosmos? What, indeed, apart from the grace of our Lord Jesus Christ? Christians are distinguished by the conviction that we do here have a window through, a clearing in being, which enables us to trust that at heart being *is* gracious.[11]

Here, above all, we shall find the truth exemplified that the best commentary on the Lord's Prayer is the Lord himself in his life and death. When we hold in our minds the constant images of horror in today's world as we are bold to say 'Our Father', we must also hold in our minds that other image of horror when Jesus hung on the cross, the victim of the world's vileness and cruelty. Then he was bold to say 'Father'. He said, 'Father, forgive them, for they know not what they do' and 'Father, into thy hands I commend my spirit'; and we have seen how, in that cry, the dying Lord's mind drew from the memories of the psalms but, even at that last moment, added to the psalmist's words the instinctive 'Father'.

If the word 'Father' in this sense presents us with a challenge, we find the answer to the challenge in the experience of Jesus himself. Here was no withdrawn religious teacher nourishing a comforting illusion about the nature of reality because he had never encountered it in its ruthless aspects. On the contrary, we have in Jesus one whose whole life was an exposure to ruthless reality. Even if, as we have judged, he had the joy of a secure and loving home, he appears to have shouldered early on the difficult task of caring for his mother and for younger brothers and sisters in a fatherless home. His stories reveal his sharp personal awareness of what the poverty line meant. He knew the price of sparrows in the market-place, and the emergency when a coin was lost. A peasant's lot in a sub-province of the Roman empire was harsh.

It was a life, moreover, in which there was constant exposure to the cruelty of men and governments. The cross Jesus carried to Golgotha was not the first he had seen. Rome used that long-drawn out agony of public execution at focal points of public movement and assembly to discourage rebellion. Once, after an unsuccessful revolt, the Galilean roads had been lined with crosses each bearing its load of writhing or putrescent flesh. If Jesus knew nothing of television's garnering of the world's agony for our living-rooms, he also did not have the flickering screen set between him and ruthless reality. For him it was starkly present.

This was the human life that Jesus shared with others in Galilee. There was his other life that was not shared, the life that was his because he was Messiah, the 'Sent One' of God. That life led him early to face a destiny of suffering and agonizing death in early manhood. The picture by Holman Hunt of Jesus stretching tired arms as he rested for a moment from work at the carpenter's bench and forming in shadow the Man Crucified may not be to our artistic taste today, but it vividly sets forth a truth. From early in his ministry Jesus faced the destiny that he revealed to the shocked Peter at Caesarea Philippi. The cross was not something that suddenly emerged as unexpected tragedy; it was recognized to be both the inevitable human result of the challenge that he offered to men and the will of God for him. The consequence for our thinking about the challenge of the word 'Father' is plain. When Jesus prayed to the Father, and taught his followers to do likewise, he knew to what ruthless reality the Father was drawing him. This emancipates the use of the word from any accusation that it could only be used by one who had not faced what I have called 'ruthless reality'. In facing it he was bold to say that it was not final reality. The final reality was Fatherhood.

Another challenge which the word 'Father' presents to us concerns the character of our prayers. If we take the word 'Father' seriously it controls the whole content and character of our prayer. We have seen this in a measure in reverse when examining the negative side of Jesus' teaching about prayer, when he forbade vain repetitions, the rattling off of innumerable phrases, and all thinking that we shall be heard for our much speaking. That mode of praying revealed clearly the underlying idea that those who used it had of the character of God or the gods. Our praying by contrast must reveal plainly our understanding of God as Father. The only prayers that a Christian can utter are those which can be addressed to the Father.

Since Jesus took a human relationship to bring this home to us, we can readily use another human relationship to exemplify it. Are there not people to whom you could never make a mean suggestion? Their integrity is such that there are things that you could never say to them. Their character rather than your own determines what you say. So it is surely with our heavenly Father.

Or it should be. The tragedy of not a little of the worshipping tradition of the church has been that it has not taken seriously enough that single word 'Father' as controlling all our prayer. Wonderful as the heritage of the English-speaking world is in the Book of Common Prayer, at times in some of those match-lessly-phrased collects you catch more the vision of a Tudor despot who has to be wheedled than one of a caring Father. The best you could say of them is that the emphasis is on our creaturely dependence rather than on the child-Father relationship.

More seriously, the things for which we have prayed when we have not held the word 'Father' steadily before our eyes have often been unworthy. This issue arose sharply for Christian men during the Second World War. There was a genuine feeling that in the First World War prayers for victory had often been jingoistic and even blasphemous. It seemed as though men had thought there was a German God and a British God, for the same prayers could not have been addressed to the same deity. Not only was the God addressed incapable of being thought of as the Father of all men; it was difficult to think that he had been conceived of as Father at all. He was some primitive tribal god of battles. What we came to see, with painful struggles (and not a few accusations of lack of patriotism addressed to men like Archbishop William Temple), was that the only prayer for victory that could at all be justified was for such an issue of the world struggle as would be for the most lasting and universal human benefit. That could rightly be claimed to be the issue that a father would desire if a bitter struggle were to break out amongst his sons. He would not yearn for the crushing of one by the other – even if the victorious one were much more in the right – but for such an outcome as would be best for them both.

So in the most critical period in the world's life for our generation we saw how the word 'Father' must control all our praying. It must no less control our personal petitions. We can only pray as Christian men and women for those things which a Father will desire to give.

In the crudest sort of area we all recognize this. Few of us would think that we could pray for vengeance on those who had done us harm. That we do not think that is a measure of what Jesus' teaching about the Father has done to our religion. The psalmists saw nothing wrong in following words of ecstatic praise and thanksgiving with words of vehement prayer for the discomfort and destruction of their enemies. But when we hear of a Christian leader who had been saying some forthright and unpalatable things receiving a postcard reading, 'I am praying fervently for your death: I have been successful in three other cases', we see such a happening as being in the realm of the pathological and the grotesque.

Are we always as alert in less crude areas? Do we take seriously enough the word of Jesus about the Father knowing what we have need of before we ask? At first glance that would seem to make prayer futile. We must again interpret the teaching of Jesus about prayer by his practice. He spent long times in prayer to the Father who knew what he had need of before he asked. His meaning, therefore, when we put his precept alongside his practice, must surely be that our prayer should have the simplicity and trust of a child opening mind and heart to an understanding father. That, and not frantic beseechings as to an indifferent or forgetful despot, must be the tone and character of Christian prayer. The moment that in language or feeling the shadow of the despotic deity falls upon our prayer we have moved far from that intimate speaking to a Father which is the heart of prayer for Jesus. As Dr George Caird has put it, Jesus 'transformed the Fatherhood of God from a theological doctrine into an intense and intimate experience; and he taught his disciples to pray with the same family intimacy.'[12]

In Matthew's version, which has been that taken into the devotional life of the church, the reading is 'Our Father'. (Luke gives the simple, direct 'Father' (Abba), which can be seen in the modern translations and revisions). This may be due to the characteristically Hebrew piety and reverence of the author of the first gospel, or to the fact that it was early adapted for liturgical use, that is, for saying by a number of people together. However this may be, certainly as it stands this plural is a striking and fitting interpretation of the whole prayer. It is striking because it immediately follows the command to 'go into a room by yourself, shut the door, and pray to your Father who is there in the secret place'. The injunction to go on your own to the private place and there pray '*Our* Father' illuminates this whole pattern prayer. As John Huxtable has finely said, 'No man is ever less alone than when he prays in secret.'[13] Nor is his company only his heavenly Father. God is like his servant Joseph of old when he says, 'Ye shall not see my face, except your brother be with you.'[14] None of us can approach the heavenly Father as an only child, whatever the substance of our prayer may be.

It is when we remember that we address the Father of all men that we shall get our prayers right. When we begin 'Our Father' all for which we ask is controlled by the one addressed, and as we say the word 'Our' we know that we cannot ask for anything which is not for the good of our brother as well as for our own good.

We must nevertheless be careful how we use the words 'Father of all men'. The phrase 'The Fatherhood of God and the brotherhood of men' has been much advanced in this century as providing an adequate creed and basis for conduct. That such a phrase, rightly understood, has its roots in the Bible and Christian revelation must not be denied, but the right understanding of the phrase is quite essential.

We tend to think of the Fatherhood of God in some such way as this: since God made the world and all that is in it, and specially created man for a particular role in that creation, all men have sprung from God. In this sense he has begotten them and they are all his sons.

In fact this is not the way in which the Bible understands the Fatherhood of God. It is something much less general and diffuse than that. It is particular, warm and personal. It has to do not with creation, but with loving redemption. Sonship is not a fact of nature; it is a gift of grace and a living relationship.

Immediately we are aware of the perils of such a statement. Is there not grave moral danger in any limitation of the universality of God's Fatherhood? It has been recorded that some slave-owners on the American cotton-plantations refused to allow their slaves to be baptized on the grounds that they would then be children of God and have to be treated as such. Could any application of Christian teaching be more perverse than that? But in today's world we can readily understand the fear sensitive men must feel at any suggestion that would limit the universal Fatherhood of God. In the hands of evil men could this not have been used to support Hitler's destruction of European Jewry; might it not be held to underpin the South African doctrine of apartheid?

The answer to this is that the universal Fatherhood of God rests on too weak a foundation to restrain men from these enormities if it be grounded only on the notion that all life owes its origin to God the creator and therefore in that sense all men are God's sons. Jesus does not thus speak of the Father. God to him was not the distant creator who must be held to have made all men, but a known and caring Father, one to be addressed with the familiar and intimate Abba. This was his experience of God. When he taught his followers to use the same word when they too spoke to God, in the words of Professor Joachim Jeremias, 'Jesus gave them a share in his relationship to God.'[15]

Relationship is here the key word. To be a son of God in the Bible is to have an actual and living relationship with him. Professor C. H. Dodd has sought to compass this essential distinction between a general sense of God as Father of mankind and the particular sense by which God calls some his sons in the paradoxical sentence, 'God is the "Father" of all men, but not all men are his "sons".'[16] 'Son' in this sense in the New Testament always means one who has been drawn into a conscious and chosen relationship with God, who not only is the Father, *but is known to be the Father*. One of the beatitudes gives us the clue; 'How blest are the peacemakers; God shall call them his sons.'[17] Those who make peace are joined with God in his activity; they are part of the firm of 'God and Sons'.

Here, in fact, and not in some diffuse sense of God's general fatherhood of mankind will be found the moral dynamic to treat all men rightly. To join in God's seeking and caring activity, an activity which knows no vestige of limitation, is the characteristic way of life of those who have learned from Jesus what it means to say 'Abba'. For such men and women the Fatherhood of God is not an abstract idea, which may be flabbily sentimental, but an experienced reality. It is a reality which compels a determined attempt to make that experience so real that all men shall be drawn home to know the Father and actually to live as sons.

NOTES

1. Luke 11.1 (NEB)
2. Andrew Young, *The Poetic Jesus*, SPCK 1971, p. 4.
3. Young, op. cit., p. 68.
4. George Adam Smith, *The Forgiveness of Sins*, Hodder & Stoughton 1904, p. 72.
5. Mark 14.36 (RSV)
6. Rom. 8.15–16 (RSV)

7. Gal. 4.6 (RSV)

8. Ernst Lohmeyer, *The Lord's Prayer*, Collins 1965, p. 35.

9. T. W. Manson, *The Sayings of Jesus*, SCM Press 1949, p. 168.

10. Ps. 103.13 (AV)

11. J. A. T. Robinson, *The Difference in Being a Christian Today*, Collins Fontana 1971, p. 29.

12. G. B. Caird, *St Luke* (The Pelican Gospel Commentaries), Penguin 1963, p. 152.

13. John Huxtable, *The Faith That Is In Us*, Independent Press 1953, p. 59.

14. Gen. 43.3 (AV)

15. Joachim Jeremias, *The Prayers of Jesus*, SCM Press 1967, p. 63.

16. C. H. Dodd, *The Epistle to the Romans* (Moffatt New Testament Commentary), Hodder & Stoughton 1932, p. 131.

17. Matt. 5.9 (NEB)

3

THE HEAVENLY FATHER

When Yuri Gagarin, the Russian astronaut, returned from his amazing journey in outer space Nikita Khruschev made a strange atheistic boast. It was to the effect that Gagarin's exploit had finally finished religion, and demonstrated what an unbased superstition it is. Had not the brave Russian space-man been up there, and combed the heavens and found no God sitting on his throne?

It was grotesque to the point of silliness, yet it represented a point on which modern Christians are somewhat touchy. In terms of the theme of this chapter we might say that many present-day Christians are happiest when least is said about 'who art in heaven'. 'If there's a God in heaven' is a colloquialism that we could well do without, for such phrases are tied up with a cosmic geography that is out of date, which has been discredited and abandoned in rational thought for centuries but still lingers on in a somewhat shame-faced way in the popular imagery of religion.

The trouble with this phrase, however, is not simply that it awakens all the debate about the 'God-up-there' and 'God-out-there' images against which Bishop John Robinson strove in *Honest to God*. Even if we cope with that we are still left with the problem of what thinkers call the transcendence of God. A simple definition of transcendence which would not be far from the mark would be 'that which is beyond the human'. Man today is very unsure about that. If he is a religious man in any degree he probably has no real difficulty about the thought of an immanent God, a God, that is, who is at work within ourselves, or even at work through his Spirit in the whole universe. He can believe in what Matthew Arnold called 'the enduring power, not ourselves, which makes for righteousness'.[1] But to think of God as transcendent, as beyond and surpassing all that is human, is something that modern man finds a great deal harder.

But the God whom Jesus revealed to men was not just a God at work within them. He transcended humanity as well as working within it. He was revealed as transcendent in the plain dictionary meaning of the term; he was far beyond our highest thought of him. Jesus showed us that our highest thought about him was to centre on the word 'Father'. But God's transcendence is not only seen in the inability of our thought to comprehend him, but in being 'beyond' us as well as beyond our highest good.

This whole element in Jesus' revelation of God is symbolized by this phrase in the Lord's Prayer, 'who art in heaven'. It is questionable whether it formed part of the original prayer. Possibly that is to be found in Luke's abbreviated form, and in Matthew we have some adaptation of it to worshipping use. It would have been natural for Matthew's gospel, the most Jewish of the four, to have supplied the phrase from the customary language of the evangelist's worshipping tradition. But, as Floyd Filson puts it, 'If Luke is closer to the wording that Jesus taught, Matthew is faithful to the meaning.'[2] 'The heavenly Father' is a phrase of Jesus of Nazareth, and when he uses the word 'Father' of God there must be no doubt that it is the picture of the heavenly Father that he has in mind. This is not the attempt of an over-fussy reverence to take away the bold intimacy of the word 'Abba' that Jesus set upon his disciples' lips; it is a true interpretation of what the word 'Father' so used meant to Jesus, and therefore what it must mean to those who followed him in life and prayer.

We must interpret the phrase not in relation to our fears of constructing a 'God out there' in whom we cannot believe, or our tendency to reduce God to some vital spiritual force only working within us, but by what we find in the rest of the gospels. When we do this we find that some of the apparent problems that the phrase seems to raise for us today are simply not there.

In the gospels, to say that God is in heaven does not put him at a distance. What, in fact, could be more absurd than that Jesus who came to make God near to men, to be Immanuel, God with us, should teach them to pray to a God at a distance? It would be a contradiction of his whole purpose. More than that, to teach men to come boldly to God with the word 'Father' on their lips, and this in its day-to-day form (as we have seen) and then add, as it were, 'but remember that this God is infinitely distant from you, away in the heavens' would be to leave men bewildered. Since the stark brevity of Jesus' prayer is intended to strip away confusion and perplexity from men's minds we can be certain that this could not have been Jesus' intention. The gospel writers speak of his great message being that the kingdom of God was 'at hand', or near. Matthew's actual phrase (it means the same thing, but shows the characteristic Jewish reverence in avoiding naming the name of God) is 'the kingdom of heaven'. Heaven is at hand, near!

No doubt in Jesus' day there was a particular set of pictures or images that religious people had, and one of them was of God seated in the highest heaven. Simpler people would understand the picture in a very literal way, and since they were not bothered by any sophisticated need to reconcile opposites, managed without difficulty to combine this with the thought of God drawing near to them. Their living faith was none the worse for their literalism.

Such a picture, nevertheless, is not part of the real teaching of Jesus. His message was that God was near, and the experience of his reign, his kingdom, was found in the midst of life. So we find that when he talks, as he often does, of his heavenly Father he is not giving God's address but describing his character. Think of another sentence from the Sermon on the Mount that contains the prayer we are studying: 'Be ye therefore perfect, even as your Father which is in heaven is perfect.'[3] Here is the clue. We are not being told where God is, but what and who he is – and this is a very different matter indeed.

It should not be difficult for us to grasp this essential distinction. The word 'heavenly' in colloquial speech is used not to describe some position in space but to speak of perfection. If we say that we have had a heavenly holiday it does not mean that some enterprising travel agent has begun package tours in outer space; it means that we had a perfect holiday. 'Heavenly' in such colloquial speech is a synonym for 'perfect', and the best way of understanding the opening of the Lord's Prayer, delivering it from the unhelpful spatial associations of the word 'heaven', is to interpret it as 'Our perfect Father'.

Emphatically this has a certain effect of 'distancing' God from us, not by putting him 'up there' in a cloud, but by stressing that he is the perfect Father. The intimacy of 'Abba' has been boldly translated by some writers as 'Daddy'. This would convey the human naturalness of the usage: what it must not suggest is that he is a Daddy who will indulge and spoil us. Most of all, it must not suggest that his indulgence of us is because he is no very great moral shakes himself. 'Our Father who art in heaven', 'Our perfect Father', gives us the boldness of intimacy without the dangers of over-familiarity. Nothing could more impoverish us than an unholy idea of God. 'Who art in heaven' delivers 'Our Father' from the gross misinterpretation of 'Our indulgent Daddy, who knows us so well that he is bound to excuse anything that we have been doing.' It tells us that we have been given boldness to approach the Holy Father with intimacy, but that does not make him less holy.

Once again we gain our best understanding if we interpret the Lord's Prayer by the Lord himself. How intimately he drew near to men, never standing apart from them in any activity of life, but how holy he remained. His understanding of his friends never for one moment becomes that weakening indulgence that Amy Carmichael of Dohnavur pithily portrayed as 'How loving so-and-so is! *She* always understands me.'[4] In this sense Jesus remained heavenly when he lived on earth.

Thus we see that the phrase, so apparently unattractive and unhelpful to the man who prays the Lord's Prayer today, in fact supplies a corrective to a potential error in our understanding of the Fatherhood of God. The very fact that fatherhood as a whole has been in some degree sentimentalized in our century might unconsciously distort for us what Jesus taught.

Not only does 'who art in heaven' supply this needed corrective, but it enlarges our whole conception of the heavenly Father in a way that is strengthening to both faith and hope.

There is an ancient Jewish prayer which begins, 'Our Father, Our King'. To this our reaction today is likely to be, to say, 'Now which? Make up your mind. Either we are to think of God as Father, or as King. You can't have it both ways.' But in a real way you can, and you must if the word 'Father' is to contain its full promise. If the word 'Father' gives us intimacy in prayer, the word 'King' – represented in part in the Lord's Prayer by the phrase 'who art in heaven' – gives us confidence. We need both intimacy and confidence in our prayers. It is because God is the heavenly Father, because the whole world owes its origin and ongoing existence and life to him, and he is the perfect Father who wills that at the last all things shall find their perfection and true life in him, that we can find confidence in him to whom we pray. He 'is able to do exceeding abundantly above all that we ask or think'[5] – being the *heavenly* Father.

So understood, the phrase 'who art in heaven' is not a grabbing back of the glorious intimacy encouraged by Jesus teaching us to say 'Abba' – 'Father, dear Father'. On the contrary, it tells us the kind of Father with whom we can have this amazing intimacy, and the confidence we can have that the petitions which follow in the prayer are addressed not just to someone who,

34

being loving, would like to answer them, but someone who can do so and wills to do so.

I risk irreverence to make this point as clear as I can. The phrase 'who art in heaven' is not a soaring away from this earth to some idealized realm. It says that the Father to whom we pray can 'deliver the goods'. He is the heavenly Father.

More illumination on this phrase can be found in a sentence Matthew records Jesus as speaking towards the end of his earthly ministry. It is a strange one. 'Do not call any man on earth "father"; for you have one Father, and he is in heaven.'[6] Again, the heavenly Father. But what can such a sentence mean? The whole point of calling God 'Father' is that this is a word with an earthly equivalent. We know from a good earthly father something of the content that we can give to the word, and from that definite point of experience try to extend that picture towards perfection as far as we can. It is because we call someone on earth 'father', and can try to 'step up' the power of this a thousand-fold, that the word is so helpful to us.

Jesus was not forbidding a man to call his real father by that name, which of course he must do. He was referring to the use of the word as a term of deference, and challenging the fondness of some of the Pharisees for being greeted in that way. What he was saying was this: when you use the word religiously save it for God himself, for in faith 'you have one father, and he is in heaven'.

More was at issue than any Pharisaic love of men's reverence. Jesus was speaking of those who were apt to put their religious stress on quite a different kind of fatherhood than that of the heavenly Father. 'Abraham is our father',[7] they would say, and by this would mean that they were very special people with a unique religious ancestry and destiny. The proof of this was to be found in their fathers. They were right; they did belong to a special people, the children of Abraham whom God had chosen to be the vehicle of his revelation of himself. This was being misinterpreted as a choice to be favourites, and they were preening themselves on being spiritual aristocrats with very special fathers.

Seeing this danger, Jesus warned them with a brutal frankness that matched the size of the moral danger of the attitude. They were to reserve the word 'Father' in the spiritual realm for God himself, and remember that he is the Father who is in heaven. That meant that he is the Father of every man under heaven, even if (as we have seen) not all men yet know themselves to be his sons.

By this sentence, which interprets this phrase from the Lord's Prayer, we are bidden abandon all insular pride in religion. For those who were always priding themselves on having Abraham for their father tended subtly but really to think that because of that God was specially their Father, too, much more than he was anyone else's Father.

The words 'who art in heaven' are an enlarging and challenging phrase. The phrase delivers us from spiritual 'little Englandism' or 'God's Own Countryism'. It was not only the Pharisees, or the Hebrew people, who had this temptation towards an insular pride in their understanding of God. It is from what is natural, joy in our own land and people, that such a perversion of true religion can readily come. We can think that we have, and (even worse) deserve, a special relationship with God.

From all this the phrase 'who art in heaven' delivers us. This is no territorial or tribal God that we address. Only those who know his Son may fully realize his Fatherhood, and be bold to cry 'Abba, Father', but it is still true that all men are his sons, and as we pray to him we must realize this.

Far from this phrase having only the disadvantage of an outmoded world view clinging to it, rightly understood it delivers us, reach upon reach, from those misunderstandings of living religion which would make faith impossible for us. It stops us cutting our concept of God down to human size by reminding us of his transcendence. It prevents us sentimentalizing his Fatherhood so as to evacuate it of holiness. It reminds us of the power of our God, and that he is Lord of all the earth and Father not of our nation but of every nation under heaven.

It is the heavenly Father to whom Jesus bids us pray, and this is not to modify, far less annul, the intimacy with which he bids us pray, but to increase the wonder that we can so speak to the Father who is also the heavenly King.

NOTES

1. Matthew Arnold, *Literature and Dogma*, 1873.
2. Floyd V. Filson, *The Gospel According to St Matthew*, A. & C. Black 1960, p. 95.
3. Matt. 5.48 (AV)
4. Frank Houghton, *Amy Carmichael of Dohnavur*, SPCK 1953, p. 343.
5. Eph. 3.20 (AV)
6. Matt. 23.9 (NEB)
7. John 8.39

4

HALLOWING THE NAME

If we have retained any sensitivity at all in our relationship with other people most of us get spasms of remorse when we suddenly realize that all our talk has been about ourselves and our concerns. The remorse may be merely social, that we have failed in good manners, or it may be genuinely moral, that we have failed to be what we should have been in our personal relationships. For a moment we stand back and look at what we have been doing. We have met someone and poured out all the ghastly things that have been happening to us, and how awful we felt on Monday morning, and wasn't it strange that Mrs So-and-So should have said such and such about us, and (looking forward) where we are planning to go for our holidays ... and then it dawns on us what we are doing, and you can almost hear the gears grind as we crash into reverse while still in full career and we murmur, composing our features into a grotesque parody of fervent interest, 'But tell me about yourself!'

The order has already given us away. It is our worries, our concerns, our plans that obsess us; the person to whom we are talking is merely a convenient pair of ears. And in our moments of sensitive insight we know that when we are like that we are not having any genuine personal relationships at all. If, tragically, we become like that all the time, and all sensitivity dies, we begin to shrink and shrivel.

Jesus knew that it could be like that in prayer. Prayer, too, like conversation, could be merely an extension of our egotism; it could be our self-concern projected on to a religious screen. We can chatter on about our needs and anxieties, our worries and fears. Jesus, knowing this danger, dealt with it when he gave the pattern prayer to his followers.

In effect he showed them that the pattern did not consist only of getting the right things into the prayer, but getting them into the right order and therefore the right relationship to one another. It is the precise function of a pattern to get things into effective order. Right order is a part of right praying.

This is not to say that all our prayers must be mapped out correctly and presented in disciplined formation. That would indeed be to cancel out all that is implied by the bidding to call God 'Father'. But just as the wise person concentrates his mind in conversation on the person he is talking to and not on himself, so the man who would pray aright concentrates upon God before moving on to any requests arising from his personal situation.

So the first petition in the Lord's Prayer is: 'Hallowed be thy name'. It centres upon God. Yes, but what is it saying? For many of us it is just a godly sound, rather like the Gloria at the end of psalm or canticle. Does it mean something precise? Can we attach a definite and helpful meaning to it?

In facing the degree to which 'hallowed' does not convey a precise meaning to our minds today I consulted seven of the modern translations of the New Testament to see how they had dealt with this problem, for one of the major purposes of those translations (in which our century has been so prolific) has been to remove archaisms and restore freshness of impact to the New Testament message.

The word has not, of course, passed wholly out of use. We might say of the church where we were married that it had hallowed associations for us. Would we attach any precise meaning to that? It is not a word that comes readily to our lips.

Six of the translations I consulted recognized this. They use

39

phrases like 'may your name be kept holy' or 'revered' or 'honoured'. This unanimity amongst the six in avoiding the use of the word 'hallowed' makes it all the more striking that the New English Bible, the only official translation prepared for the churches other than Roman Catholic of these islands, retains the word 'hallowed'. This retention, moreover, is in a translation deliberately committed to the avoidance of the archaic.

Reflection may make us grateful for the caution of the New English Bible translators. Even an unusual word, especially if it be regarded as inviting us to grapple with its meaning, is better than any words that thin out the meaning of the original. All the other phrases, however well-intentioned their simplifying and modernizing may be, appear to do this.

There is another word, as well as 'hallowed', with which we need to grapple if we are to grasp the full meaning of the phrase. There is nothing in the faintest degree archaic or obviously difficult about that word; it is 'name', a word that we use constantly. We all feel that we know what it means, but we probably do not appreciate its full force here. That rests on what the name meant to the Hebrew mind. 'A rose by any other name would smell as sweet' summarizes our common understanding of what a name is. It is a label that we use for our convenience; in no degree does it affect the reality. But it cannot be too strongly stressed that such an idea is entirely contrary to what the name meant to the Hebrew. For him the name *was* the reality.

Constantly this appears in the Old Testament. It will be sufficient to mention three outstanding moments. One is when Jacob, returning home after his long exile to face the expected wrath of Esau, the brother whom he had cheated, wrestled with the mysterious stranger at the brook Jabbok. His demand was that the stranger should tell him his name, for Jacob suspected that at this moment of crisis in his life, when death might be awaiting him, he was wrestling with the divine reality. To know the name would be to know the reality.

At another high moment of Old Testament history the same point emerged. When Moses heard God speak to him from the burning bush, and commission him to liberate his enslaved people, he wanted to know the name of the God who sent him. To know the name would be to know the power.

It is there, too, in the Ten Commandments, the second of which is a specific command regarding the name of God. 'Thou shalt not take the name of the Lord thy God in vain; for the Lord will not hold him guiltless that taketh his name in vain.'[1]

Again we can look to Dr Manson to sum the point up: 'For Hebrew thought the name is not a mere word. It is in a sense the person so named. To know God's name is in a real sense to know God.'[2]

A notion like this may seem remote and unreal to us. Some of its force for the Hebrew may come home to us through a simple illustration. Suppose you had to make a sad journey back to the family home because someone very dear to you had died. It would be the kind of journey made in some turmoil of mind and emotions. If you were told, 'You'll be met at the station', it would be a help. But if you were told, 'John will meet you at the station', and John was a person on whose calm and strong personality you could lean, what a difference that would make! There is all the difference between the vague general and the splendid particular. For the Hebrew it was in that sense that the name of God gave concreteness and sustaining reality to the very thought of God. God was not some vague, diffused notion that somewhere, somehow, within things in general, there was a general divine presence: God was a reality, the kind of reality that possessed a name.

To reckon with this different way of thinking about the word 'name' enormously fills out the first petition in the Lord's Prayer. It is not the 'name' of God in our poor notion of the meaning of the word that is being talked about: it is nothing less than the reality of God.

Perhaps it becomes clearest when we ask what is being done

when the name of God is not being hallowed. When that happens, when in the words of the commandment, that name is being 'taken in vain', what is being described? Most of us would expect some distasteful blasphemy, some succession of expletives using the word 'God' as a swear-word. This is distressing to the believer, and is to be condemned for its irreverence; but it is something much bigger than this that the commandment was about. To take the name of God in vain was not primarily to blaspheme by the lips, but by action.

You could in fact picture circumstances in which a man was blaspheming verbally quite appallingly while serving God very splendidly. Suppose a child were trapped in some hole, the sides of which were caving in. A man of total rectitude of speech might stand by too gripped by fear to do anything about it, but a rough fellow might plunge down and work away in danger of his life to release the child, while all the time uttering the most blood-curdling blasphemies, with nervous tension working on a lifetime's stupid habit of common swearing. It would be the man of blameless speech whose fear was making him take the name of the God and Father of all little ones in vain. The technical blasphemer would be hallowing the name of God.

For what is it that we mean – with this understanding of 'name', signifying the reality – when we pray 'Hallowed be thy name'? A great part of what we are saying can be paraphrased by some such sentence as this: 'God, be God to me and to my world.' A child's hymn runs

> *Jesus, friend of little children,*
> *Be a friend to me.*

That is to say, 'I know what Jesus is like, but I want it to happen to me, I want Jesus to be like that to me.' So in the prayer 'Hallowed be thy name' we are saying 'We know, God, what you are like – now let us see it in action.' I put this again with some deliberate irreverence for I want to break through our pious notion of this part of the prayer.

It is in what the grammarians call the passive mood, and this was deliberately to cast a bold thought in reverent terms. So out of consideration and courtesy we might say to the housewife who has prepared the meal, 'Let's have dinner now' rather than 'Serve the dinner.' So the Jew thought it right that the one praying should not command God, but say 'let something be' rather than 'do' that thing.

Whatever the reverence of the outward form might fitly be, the content is the same. 'Father, be holy' is the real meaning of this petition. But surely, it may be objected, that is just what God is; what we understand by holiness *is* the God and Father of Jesus Christ. But it remains true that the honest prayer of every man must be that God's holiness will be shown in action.

As the cross drew near Jesus prayed, 'Father, glorify thy name.'[3] In that day 'glorify' and 'hallow' would mean the same. Jesus uses the imperative. He asks simply that God should do it, that he should sweep into action. So Jesus prayed on the first Palm Sunday, 'Glorify thy name,' 'Father, act now'. He made the pattern prayer his own, and if God were to glorify, to hallow his name in the days that lay ahead we know what this meant for us, *and what Jesus knew that it meant.* When Jesus prayed that God would be God, that he would go into action, he recognized the consequences for himself. When he prayed thus he offered himself. To pray for the hallowing of God's name in this meant the commitment of himself to that hallowing as well as God's direct action.

This is always implied in this petition. We cannot pray 'Hallowed be thy name' without a dedication of ourselves in some measure to the hallowing of God's name, that is, to the honouring of the reality of God in the world. If God's action is sought, it can never be separated from human response. We cannot ask for God to be at work, hallowing his name, being the Holy Father in action in the world, while being idle ourselves. Such idleness divests our prayer of all integrity. Emphatically we cannot pray that God's name may be hallowed while working against the purposes of God. That is far ranker blasphemy than the most repellent string of curses using the name of God for their raw material.

This principle is not something peculiar to prayer and the life of faith and obedience. It is a principle that runs right through human life. To express some desire for human betterment even in ordinary conversation, not in prayer, and withhold your own effort for bringing it about reduces what you say to idle chatter. If a man says, 'I think old people ought to be better cared for' and does nothing to make the lot of his own old parents easier, he is in this just a useless gabbler. Human desires imply human action. How much more then do our prayers to our heavenly Father imply commitment to bringing about that for which we pray?

So while the first petition in the Lord's Prayer centres upon God and upon the desire to see his holiness in action in the world, it boomerangs back upon ourselves. To pray thus is always to make a dedication as well as a petition.

The challenging implications of this petition may be taken a stage further. In studying separately the phrases of the Lord's Prayer we must never wrest them from their context. What is this name of God which is to be hallowed? It is not 'Yahweh', the ancient name of God cherished amongst the Israelites from the earliest days. It is 'Abba', 'Father'. This is the name that is to be hallowed. 'Father, be Father to us'; 'Father, let the world come to know and honour your Fatherhood' – in such phrases can we see much of the content of 'Hallowed be thy name'. It is a prayer for the universal manifestation and realization of God's fatherly care.

It is from this that the challenging consequence flows. As Ernst Lohmeyer puts it, 'the hallowing of God's name "Father" also means the hallowing of all those to whom he is Father'.[4] Just as we have seen that we are called to pray 'Our Father', even when praying personally and individually, that we cannot,

44

in fact, leave our brother outside the locked door of our private oratory, so we must see that to pray for the hallowing of the name of God which is 'Father' involves consequences for our attitude to our brother. If we hold God's name as Father to be sacred, to be that which we must hallow, we must hold all his children to be sacred, too. What may appear to be the most ethereal of the phrases of the Lord's Prayer, with its specially 'religious' word, 'hallowed', embedded in it, becomes searching in regard to political and social justice.

It follows from this that the real concern of the Christian man, the man who prays 'Our Father', with the society in which he lives will be deeper than anxiety about verbal profanity and blasphemy, however much they may offend his sense of decency and reverence. His real concern must not be with the puerile blasphemies of the underground press or the way-out television play, but with whether God's nature as Father is being reflected in the character of the society in which he lives. Is it the kind of society in which the young, the weak, the old are specially cared for? Is the system by which it is organized one that increases human happiness, or one which profits only one section of the community? Is it a society in which to be human matters far more than to which ethnic group or social class you belong? These questions are not to be seen as merely the stock-in-trade of the progressive; they are some of the central questions when we are concerned about the hallowing of the name of God. For is it not the nature of a father to want to see the less fortunate or strong of his children receiving particular care, to be concerned for the happiness of all his children rather than the wealth of a few of them, and to make no distinction between them on artificial grounds? Any father feels his fatherhood to be fulfilled when his family live happily and affectionately together. The heavenly Father will seek no different hallowing of his fatherly name.

NOTES

1. Exod. 20.7 (AV)
2. T. W. Manson, *The Sayings of Jesus*, SCM Press 1949, p. 168.
3. John 12.28 (AV)
4. Ernst Lohmeyer, *The Lord's Prayer*, Collins 1965, p. 82.

5

THE COMING KINGDOM

Any attentive reader of the Bible sees that the main characteristic of Hebrew poetry was not rhyme, or even (so much as ours) rhythm, but the saying of almost the same things in slightly different words, as

> Thy word is a lamp unto my feet, and
> a light unto my path.[1]

The ingenious preacher may make a distinction, suggesting that the first is the hand-held lamp for one's next step, and the light the distant shining that determines the goal, but, however edifying such distinctions may be, they belong to the realm of imagination rather than scholarship.

In some instances nonetheless, as well as a parallelism (to give the device its usual name) there is a development, or a fresh image introduced, as in

> The Lord is thy keeper:
> The Lord is thy shade upon thy right hand.[2]

The two lines of poetry have the same theme-thought, God as protector, but the second line introduces a new picture.

There is poetry in the Lord's Prayer. Professor Jeremias has pointed out that

> Hallowed be thy name,
> Thy kingdom come

is poetry after this fashion. (Unusually there is a third parallel line, if we add 'Thy will be done' as Matthew but not Luke does.[3])

Our concern, of course, is not with the Lord's Prayer as a form of literature, but the literary form in which it is cast illuminates its message at this point. Here there are three parallel petitions, for the hallowing of the name of God, the coming of the kingdom of God, and the doing of the will of God. They *are* parallels moving in precisely the same direction, but they are the kind of parallels in which there is a sufficient shift in the imagery or pictures used for fresh light to be shed on what is common to all these petitions.

What is common and central is God himself. All three concentrate on God, not on ourselves. Dag Hammarskjöld sharply observed, 'Your cravings as a human animal do not become a prayer just because it is God whom you ask to attend to them.' In the pattern prayer Jesus ensures that what we offer is prayer by setting our minds and hearts on God himself, his name (which means his nature and reality), his kingdom or rule, and his will. Before we move to a single one of our needs we think upon God in his being, his authority and his purpose.

The two parallels which follow 'Hallowed be thy name' are interpretations and commentaries on it. To pray that God's kingdom may come is in another form to pray that the name of God may be hallowed, for it is best hallowed when his rule is most realized. It is still true that something further is being said, and the fulness of the interpretation being offered is only gained as we in some measure grasp what it means to pray for the coming of the kingdom of God.

The kingdom of God is a phrase which suffers from too much use rather than from becoming archaic. It could be described as the major theme of the gospels. It has been calculated that it (and its precise equivalent 'the kingdom of heaven' which Matthew especially, for reasons of reverence, uses) occurs in the first three gospels no less than 103 times. This might seem to make it easy to understand its use here in the Lord's Prayer, but as well as

48

having been much used it has been misused. This has been notably true in our century, and although the scholars recovered the biblical use of the phrase for us some decades ago it is doubtful whether the message has fully sunk into the general consciousness of the Christian community. Put simply the message is that the kingdom is not something that we bring in by human effort, no matter how consecrated or devout, but is purely God's gift to which all that we can offer is decisive acceptance.

Much Christian thinking early in this century was dominated by the thought of bringing in the kingdom of God as a form of Utopia to be realized fairly fully in the near future. It was the spiritual form of the secular optimism which rested on the notion of inevitable progress. Perhaps the best comment on this comes from Helmut Thielike in his book on the Lord's Prayer, *The Prayer that Spans the World*. It gains in force by the situation in which the words were spoken. There is a footnote on the opening page of his chapter on 'Thy Kingdom come' which reads:

> This sermon was delivered in the choir of the Church of the Hospitallers since the church itself had been reduced to pitiful ruins in the air raids immediately preceding this time. The centre of the city of Stuttgart was also totally destroyed.

Words about the kingdom spoken in such a situation have power behind them.

> We must not think of it as a gradual Christianization of the world which will increasingly eliminate evil. Such dreams and delusions, which may have been plausible enough in more peaceful times, have vanished in the terrors of our man-made misery. The nineteenth century, which brought forth a number of these dreams and dreamers, strikes us today as being an age of unsuspecting children.[4]

We must not secularize the kingdom of God in this fashion. The coming of the kingdom is the hallowing of the name of God, not the hallowing of our scientific advancement and social amelioration. Scholars today are clear that this petition in the Lord's Prayer is eschatological, that is, it has to do with the 'eschaton', the end. It is, if you like, a prayer for perfection, a perfection of God's freely accepted control over human life which is not to be expected within the time-process.

Does this mean that we are driven back to an interpretation of this petition which was very common before the nineteenth-century thinkers linked it to the idea of human progress? That earlier dominant conception, which had held sway in the Christian fellowship for a very long time, wholly linked the petition to the Second Advent of Christ. By this interpretation the kingdom had really nothing to do with this world at all; to pray 'Thy kingdom come' was to offer an entirely other-worldly prayer. We are not to interpret the eschatological emphasis being laid upon it today in this fashion. Professor Jeremias has put his finger on the difference. He draws an illuminating parallel with the ancient Aramaic prayer called the *Kaddish* which begins

> Exalted and hallowed be his great name
> in the world which he created according to his will.
> May he let his kingdom rule
> in your lifetime and in your days . . .

The parallel is only partial: there is strong contrast, too.

> The two 'Thou-petitions' are not the same as the *Kaddish*, in spite of the similar wording. There is a great difference. In the *Kaddish* the prayer is by a congregation which stands in the darkness of the present age and asks for the consummation. In the Lord's Prayer, though similar words are used, a congregation is praying which knows that the turning point has already come, because God has already begun his saving work. This congregation now makes supplication for full revelation of what has already been granted.[5]

Here is the all important difference. There is a sense in which the end has begun already. Not the Second Advent of Christ but his first coming has settled the final issue, although the interim through which we now live can be painful and tragic almost beyond bearing. 'Almost' is the word; suffering there may be, but there will not be despair for those who know Christ and his saving work. When we pray 'Thy kingdom come' we are not expressing a wistful longing for life to move to a different and happier goal; we are praying for the consummation of that which has already been determined. Moreover, and this is of great significance, because it has already been determined, because there is a present experience of the kingdom, some fuller realization does not necessarily await the full and final realization. We may look not to the theologians but to the perception of a Christian poet to guide us here. Andrew Young wrote:

> But the invocation 'Our Father' should have told the disciples that for them in some small measure the Kingdom was already come; 'Thy kingdom come' is a petition that it may spread.[6]

'Spreading' is a sounder word than 'bringing in', but even with that word we must be careful. 'Thy kingdom come' is a petition which certainly must be held to include the missionary work of Christ's church, which is often described as spreading the kingdom. But it is not something primarily that we spread, but something that God spreads. So our petition is not, 'Help us, Father, to spread your kingdom', but, 'Thy kingdom come'. The stress is upon God's initiative, not on our enterprise and activity. Human enterprise and activity there may be, but they are derivative and secondary; God's initiative is what is primary.

Jesus did not invent the phrase 'the kingdom of God'. Rabbis had begun to use it just before his coming. Naturally Jesus had to use phrases which were meaningful to his hearers. What he did was not to forge an original phrase, but to impart an original meaning. Above all, Jesus took from that phrase anything nationalistic or jingoistic, anything that was related merely to Jewish hopes and aspirations. He universalized its meaning.

When Jesus came on earth many deeply religious men believed that God's kingdom, his rule over his chosen people, was bound to be asserted before many days had passed. How could God allow his land, the land he had promised to his people, to be desecrated by pagan and tyrannical rule? This vile phase must swiftly pass, and the kingdom of God be ushered in.

There were at least three strands in this expectation. One was that the kingdom of God would be inaugurated by heroic violence. It was the way of the zealots. Jesus felt sufficiently the strength of the temptation to claim the kingdoms of the world and the glory of them by that method to have to wrestle with it beyond Jordan. Matthew suggests that it was the final, and therefore the strongest of the temptations (if we may assume that Satan knows his business well enough to keep his most devastating shot to the last). After all, it was in Jesus' boyhood that his own Galilee had been the scene of an uprising against the Romans, to cleanse it from its pollution and bring in the day of God's rule, or kingdom, over his people. It was crushed with a terrible ferocity. But at least one of the inner band of the followers of Jesus was a man who had shared those aspirations; he was called Simon the Zealot. One scholar, the late Professor S. G. F. Brandon, has even argued that Jesus himself espoused the zealot cause, and that there has been a rewriting of the history of his mission by the evangelists to ingratiate the Christian cause with the Roman authorities. It is a somewhat perverse thesis, and not one which has commended itself to many other scholars. We may note it for two reasons. One is that the argument can be advanced at all by a reputable scholar argues at least for the seriousness of the zealot belief that this way of violence was a justified way of working that God's kingdom may come. The other is that this scholarly thesis has been used to support arguments for Christian violence today as a mode of seeking the coming of the kingdom.

The best known of these arguments is that of Colin Morris in his *Unyoung Uncoloured Unpoor*,[7] in which he justifies the most brutal violence by the Zambian-based and trained guerrilla against the Smith regime in Rhodesia. The most 'respectable' ecclesiastical support for such a position came from the executive committee of the World Council of Churches when it made grants towards the liberation movements in Southern Africa. These grants were only for welfare work, but they implied a measure of support for movements avowedly violent in method (and insofar as they relieved the budgets of such movements on the welfare side, enabled more money to be spent on arms and ammunition). Here, in fact, has emerged one of the sharpest challenges to Christian conscience today. The zealots in our Lord's day could point to a long line of those in the earlier history of the people who had sought to establish the sovereignty of the Lord God over his people by might of arms. They followed in the footsteps of men like Joshua in the distant past, and the Maccabees in the recent past; they were would-be conquerors in the name of the righteousness of God.

Their modern counterparts can point to the role in our distant past of a military leader like Cromwell in the establishment of more democratic institutions in England, and our admiration of the resistance movements in Hitler-occupied Europe in the recent past. In fact the whole taking up of arms against Nazism (often by those who had espoused a Christian pacifism in the inter-war years) could be regarded as in some measure the zealot attitude. If the kingdom of God is partly, at least, justice and freedom, were we not fighting for its coming by weapons of violence from 1939–45?

We may be critical of the very ready espousing of the cause of violence by some Christians, and some Christian bodies today. There is some justification for John Huxtable's critical observation about those who are 'trigger-happy in the cause of righteousness'. They are curiously selective in the causes that they believe warrant such action; but just as the zealots of Jesus' day were surely often ardent and sensitive men who found it unbearable that tyranny should go unopposed, so our contemporary zealots often are more eager for God's kingdom of righteousness and justice to come than those who brush aside the disturbing challenge of their position. Such brushing-aside may only mean that we have not really felt through compassionate identification the agony of those who live out a lifetime seeing further and further inroads upon the tiny freedom they have, and more and more

53

barriers built against their ever sharing in the liberation that they see coming all around them.

Another strand in the Jewish expectation of the coming of God's kingdom was that of the Pharisees and those who followed their leadership. We tend to use the word Pharisee as a synonym for hypocrite, and the gospels give us plenty of warrant for doing so. Here I write of the Pharisee at his best (although the fact that they fell so readily into the hypocrisy that Jesus searingly condemned must be taken into our eventual assessment of the value of their way of working for the coming of the kingdom).

The Pharisee did not take the zealot's way. He detested the Roman tyranny as much. He had particular religious reasons for detesting it even more, for such heathen domination was not only a vile tyranny but an abominable desecration. The Promised Land was being soiled. Such pagan presence, moreover, meant inevitable religious and moral corruption for many. Nevertheless the Pharisee believed that the only way of seeking the coming of God's kingdom was by keeping God's moral law, that law which had been worked out in intricate detail by the scribes of the Pharisees to cover all the contingencies and choices of life. Let more and more of God's people accept the rule of his law and then Israel would experience his reign, his kingdom, for they would be prepared for his supernatural coming.

It has become more clear in recent years that there were other strands in the expectation of the coming of the kingdom in Jesus' day. There are traces of others especially in the birth stories in Luke's gospel, and the uncovering of the Qumran community of the Dead Sea Scrolls suggests that too ready a division of religious attitudes into the Sadducean worldly refusal to have any expectations, the Pharisees' sophisticated legalism, and the zealot activism and violence may not do justice to the complexity of the scene. Certainly in such figures in the early chapters of Luke as Elizabeth and Zacharias, Anna and Simeon, a piety is revealed which was eager and warm without being violent, and an expectation which had more substance than the dessicated gradualism of the Pharisees. The lovely songs which give such glory and beauty to the opening chapters of Luke may be later compositions in their form, but must reflect the actual devoutness of real people. Such a man as Simeon and such a woman as Anna believed that God would act to bring in his kingdom. It was a different expectation from that of the zealot or the Pharisee. Like theirs it would be a great deal nourished on that religious literature that is called apocalyptic (of which Daniel is an example in the Old Testament and Revelation in the New). Possibly they would in their simple and popular way hold more passionately the expectation of an unmistakable Day of the Lord which would usher in the kingdom which found vivid and imaginative expression in current apocalyptic writing. But if Simeon and Anna are anything to go by, their expectation did not involve taking the highly-coloured pictures of the apocalypses too literally. They, at least, saw the Day of the Lord not in a descent from the clouds but in a baby brought into the Temple by his peasant parents.

Where zealot, Pharisee and the simple believer like Simeon found common ground was in their conviction that things were in a desperate state. Their expectations of how change could come about were contrasted at many points, but their hopes were one. They hoped that there would be a Day of the Lord, a coming of the kingdom when God would take his power and reign, subduing the evil that made havoc of human happiness and above all of the life of God's chosen people.

Not many Christians will want to part company with that hope today. We, too, yearn passionately for a new deal for this world of ours. Tyranny flourishes in much of our world, as it did in the Palestine of Jesus' day. Then it was a single tyranny; today it has many forms. It ranges from the tyranny of Communist-occupied lands to the unprincipled capitalist regimes in some Latin American countries, from the racist governments of Southern Africa to (in all honesty) the tribalism of some newly independent states. Fear and brutality in these situations march hand in hand. Dark spectres of population explosion, nuclear destruction and ecological disaster shadow our spirits.

In such a situation any man with the faintest glimmering of faith is apt to cry inside himself, 'Is God going to do anything about it? Shall we see God coming as King, that is, taking control of this chaos and bringing harmony and meaning to life?' Again, some of those most agonized over the suffering of the oppressed would hasten the coming of that kingly rule of God by taking the way of violence. Others, sickened by the spread of violence and doubtful whether you can ever arrest its dread contagion, even if it be used in the cause of righteousness, put their trust just in trying to make individual men better, setting before them God's moral law, as did the Pharisee. They fervently hope that there will be time for this very gradual process to work before one or other of the threatening cosmic disasters strikes.

With these things in mind we may turn to Mark's gospel when he describes Jesus beginning to give his message to men. 'Jesus came into Galilee proclaiming the Gospel of God: The time has come; the kingdom of God is upon you . . .'[8] It is as if he had said, 'You have wanted it; you have yearned for it; you have prayed for it; you have wondered if it would ever happen. Right! It is happening now! This is the time. The kingdom of God has come upon you.'

How? Certainly there had not been any great and successful zealot uprising. As certainly there had not been any sudden mass-turning to the way of the Pharisees; their way of living life by keeping regulations seemed a plain impossibility for ordinary people. Certainly there had been no phenomenal and supernatural rending of the heavens to show that God was going to take a masterful hand in human affairs. So what had happened to justify this startling announcement?

Jesus himself had come. Just that. The great Day had dawned; the kingdom of God was upon them because Jesus himself had come amongst them.

In what sense could the coming of Jesus bring the kingdom?

The word itself tends to be misleading to us. It has almost ineradicable geographical connotations. We think of the kingdom of God as an area, as we think of the United Kingdom. But the primary meaning of the phrase in the Bible is not that, but what we today would more naturally call the kingship of God, the fact that God *is* King, that he rules. This does, of course, imply a second meaning, that he rules over something. We must not detach the thought of God's kingship from that, and make him like one of the pathetic ex-royalties on the Riviera, claiming the title of king but having neither territory nor subjects.

At the time Jesus came they thought of God as King over his people, Israel, but this basic thought had to be both extended and contracted. It had to be extended by recognizing that no true picture of God, Maker of heaven and earth, could set national limits to his reign. However much it was believed that his people had a peculiar and intimate experience of his kingship, it had to be recognized that his rule must extend over all people and all the earth. It had also to be in a sense contracted by the recognition that even in Israel his rule was very imperfectly acknowledged. Many men lived lives that simply rejected his rule. They were rebellious and disaffected subjects. Even over the lives of the best of men his reign was only partial. Nowhere did God seem to have a full and complete reign.

In Jesus he did. Here is the clue to why Jesus proclaimed that the kingdom of God had come among them. *He* had come among them, and in the territory of one heart and will, that of Jesus of Nazareth, God's reign was totally acknowledged. In that real, definite and factual sense the kingdom had come.

Once we see this clearly our prayer 'Thy kingdom come' becomes a confident cry. There is nothing of the pathos of 'wishing it might be so' about it. Christ himself, who was the total territory of the kingdom, is the ground of this sustaining confidence.

We must be careful to differentiate this from the Pharisaic belief that God's kingdom would be advanced only by slowly winning men to obey the Law of God, and thus acknowledge his sovereignty. A similar attitude may be found today in Christian groups that shun all political and social involvement in favour of 'bringing in the kingdom' by the sole means of individual evangelical conversion. This is a retreat into a personal moralism that does not face the basic moral problem of our time, which is how a man can be moral in an immoral society that controls so much of his life. A life of personal rigorous puritanism – abstention from the 'worldliness' of liquor, smoking, gambling and the rest – if linked with a contented attitude towards apartheid, the ravages of competitive capitalism and the like is but distantly related to any biblical concept of the kingdom of God. We must not move from recognition that the kingdom fully came in one heart and mind, that of Jesus of Nazareth, to the notion that our sole business is to extend its territory by the addition of more individual hearts and minds.

For one thing this is profoundly unevangelical. It does violence to the uniqueness of Christ. Christ's coming *was* divine intervention. It was the Day of the Lord, even though there was no descending on a cloud and no shaking of the heavens. It was fulfilment of the hope that God would act, and that action is now the ground of all our hope.

Once we see that God acted in Christ, and that the kingdom came in him who perfectly acknowledged the right of God to hold sway over his heart, mind and will, the hope that God's reign shall at the last be complete, and finally all enemies of human well-being will be put under his feet, rests not upon the fragile support of a human dream but the actual proof of a human life. Men saw a life that was not invaded by selfishness, greed, lust and dishonesty. Men saw a life in which self had been conquered, not aggrandized by striving for godliness. They saw a life which strangely conquered the forces which rebelled against God's kingship – for that surely should be our basic understanding of the miracles. They saw disease, mental affliction, hunger and the enmity of nature subdued and conquered by him. He healed many by his touch; he cast out devils; he fed the five thousand; he stilled the storm. Here was the kingly rule of God made visible. The time *had* come, the kingdom of God *was* among them – moving in the figure of the Man of Nazareth.

For Christian men Jesus Christ himself is the ground of an enormous hope, or rather a well-based conviction. He is, however, more than that. He is also the indication of the character of the kingdom. When we pray for the coming of the kingdom we pray for the full coming of a kingdom of the character shown by Christ. That means the ending of suffering, hunger, mental affliction, injustice, and the conquest of those forces of nature which are inimical to human life and happiness.

This does not mean that we slip by a by-way into the utopian notions of the kingdom which, as we have seen, dominated so much popular Christian thinking earlier in this century. We are delivered from them if we take seriously the fact that Christ gives us the character as well as the hope of the kingdom. That makes us face what happened to the first full incarnation of the kingdom. Men crucified him: they sought to obliterate that kingdom by destroying its territory. The coming of the kingdom must mean the conquest of demonic forces of immense and terrifying power. Here is no steady march of inevitable progress but the calling in of divine power to fight those demonic elements that destroy true human existence.

But as we pray for that divine power, that kingly force, in the petition 'Thy kingdom come', we cannot do so with folded hands, or, in the old phrase, with ungirt loins. The more we pray for the kingly power of God to be shown in the world the more we must desire to have an increased experience of it.

It may be wrong and unbiblical to speak of our bringing in or extending the kingdom of God, for right through the New Testament the stress is on the kingdom as God's gift. Gifts none the less can be rejected, and the gospels equally stress the need for man to show decisiveness in accepting the gift when it comes. The urgency of the decision to accept the gift is the most constant theme of the parables of the kingdom. The jeweller selling his whole stock swiftly to secure the priceless pearl; the dismissed estate-manager who makes friends for the future by writing down his master's debts; the tiresome woman hammering on the judge's door – all kinds of odd characters are called in to illustrate this essential urgency and decisiveness. Nothing could be more foreign to what Jesus taught about the kingdom than to suggest that a pious listlessness honours God more than a bustling activism.

The man, moreover, who has decided to claim God's gift, and experience that kingly rule in his life, is not true to the majesty of the thought of it being *God's* kingdom if he takes small and narrow views of the area of human life that that sovereignty will claim. He must venture forth into the whole of man's social and political life to see how the kingdom of God is to be realized in it. For many this will not mean playing any obviously decisive role, for they have not got their hands on the levers of power, but for all Christians it must mean the recognition that their judgments on social, industrial and political questions cannot be unaffected by the fact that they have prayed 'Thy kingdom come'. When the kingdom came in Jesus, conquest of sickness, stress, hunger, the destructive forces of nature were deeply involved. This speaks about priorities in hospital-building programmes, the situation in our mental asylums, world development, and the growing concern for ecology. And though the word we translate as 'kingdom' must not be conceived in terms of an area, it must surely be grasped as implying a community. The stress is on its being God's kingdom but it is a kingdom among men, and any kingdom is by its very nature communal and corporate. It is not just a collection of individuals unrelated to one another. To acknowledge God as King is to see your fellow-men as fellow-citizens of that kingdom, and the need for your life together to express no less acknowledgment of the kingly rule of God than your own personal life.

The point is vividly made in a tribute by William Temple in

the posthumously published *Autobiography* of Conrad Noel. It concerns an incident at the famous COPEC conference of 1924.

> A speaker had just been telling us that we must always think of the kingdom of God as the reign of God in the individual heart. I saw Conrad Noel waving his papers in the air and I called on him at once, though his name had not been handed in and I had others before me. He hurried up the platform and said only this: 'They shall come from the east and the west and shall sit down with Abraham, Isaac, and Jacob in the reign of God in the individual heart.' He then returned as hurriedly to his seat with his point effectively made.[9]

Not only the New Testament, therefore, will be in our minds when we pray 'Thy kingdom come'; the daily newspaper and the current affairs television programmes will be there as well. Our prayer is purged of easy utopianism when we remember what happened to the teacher of that prayer, but it is strengthened by the belief that the destructive forces in man's heart did not obliterate the embryonic kingdom that found its territory in the Man of Nazareth. In that strength we pray for a realization of the kingdom that must rest on the power of our kingly God and not on the inevitable progress of man's knowledge and skills.

This must not be so set over against the reign of God in the individual heart as to suggest that this latter conquest is no part of the biblical picture of the kingdom. To pray for the kingdom to come while obdurately guarding the frontiers of your own life against any royal progress of God into it is plain hypocrisy. Our belief in the kingdom of God and its final coming in its fulness rests on the existence of that kingdom in Jesus, but that conviction will be weakened or strengthened in the degree that we refuse to admit God's rule in our lives. It may well occur to us that the coming of the kingdom in the common life of mankind may be uncomfortable for us. We may not be as important as we thought we were, and some people whom we discounted may be taking over some of our privileges. Of course we want the kingdom of God to come, in the sense that we want the forces that are destroying human life and happiness to be defeated. So did the Pharisees, but when it did come they saw it as threat rather than promise. It is not a light thing to pray for the coming of the kingdom.

NOTES

1. Ps. 119.105 (AV)
2. Ps. 121.5 (AV)
3. The Authorized Version is misleading here: see modern revisions and translations.
4. Helmut Thielicke, *The Prayer that Spans the World*, James Clarke 1965, pp. 55, 60.
5. Joachim Jeremias, *The Prayers of Jesus*, SCM Press 1967, pp. 98–99.
6. Andrew Young, *The Poetic Jesus*, SPCK 1971, p. 49.
7. Epworth Press 1969.
8. Mark 1.14–15 (NEB)
9. Conrad Noel, *Autobiography* ed. Sidney Dark, J. M. Dent 1945, p. 81.

6

DOING THE WILL

A no doubt apocryphal tale records that in a country churchyard there is a tombstone bearing an inscription at once guileful and guileless.

> *Beneath this stone in hopes of Zion*
> *Doth lie the landlord of the Lion.*
> *His son keeps on the business still,*
> *Resigned unto the heavenly will.*

If true it must be accounted an early example of that modern phenomenon, the commercial. That is its guileful aspect. The guileless one is the conventionally pious phrase with which it closes.

Phrases like that were much on our forefathers' lips. 'He lived in complete submission to the will of God'; 'He resigned himself to the heavenly will'; 'His spirit was one of humble waiting upon the will of God.' Phrases like these represent an aspect of Christianity most unattractive to modern man. They speak to us of folded hands, eyes soulfully lifted towards heaven, and an abandonment of all human effort and enterprise in favour of a passive and lethargic waiting upon God's decisions and actions. Scarcely anything in the realm of religion is more repulsive to modern men than that.

Such an attitude contradicts that autonomy of man, that capacity to control his environment and to master nature and circumstance, which has been man's greatest passion and achievement. To be resigned to the heavenly will suggests that you accept destructive flooding instead of bestirring yourself to build barrages and controls, that you accept the visitation of smallpox and typhoid instead of organizing mass vaccination and innoculation, that in fact you accept disaster, disease and death instead of using every cell of the mind and every muscle and sinew of the body to fight these things.

The modern era, seen in one aspect, is the product of man's confident and sustained refusal to accept what religious men were ready to call the will of God. Since this aspect is perhaps the most encouraging side of human life to contemplate you can readily understand an instructive refusal of all that is implied by 'resigned unto the heavenly will'.

Built into the whole 'feel' of today's world is the notion that it is only as man holds fast to his autonomy, his ever-lengthening and ever-firmer grip on the forces of nature and his ever-deepening knowledge of the forces at work in his own mind, both conscious and subconscious, that human happiness will be advanced. Anything which questions this is seen as a threat, and the notion of a way of life which is religious acceptance rather than human challenge is seen as a ludicrous throw-back to a stage from which man has happily evolved.

So we must face the question whether this is the real nature of the petition in the Lord's Prayer, 'Thy will be done on earth as it is in heaven.' We are the more compelled to do this if we take seriously the guide-post for our study that Dr Manson has set up when he says that Mark 14.36 is the best commentary on this petition.[1] That verse reads: 'Abba, Father, all things are possible to thee; remove this cup from me; yet not what I will, but what thou wilt.'

As Jesus moved towards the close of his life on earth, towards the crisis of betrayal, agony and death, he reveals that the prayer which he gave to his disciples is that which he was praying all the time. 'Hallowed be thy name', he taught them to pray, and on the first day of the week that led to Calvary he prayed, 'Father, glorify (hallow) thy name.'[2] 'Thy will be done' is another phrase he set on the lips of his disciples at prayer: 'Father, not my will but thine be done,' he cried in the garden of Gethsemane. 'Forgive us ... as we forgive' was a later petition in his pattern prayer: 'Father, forgive them; for they know not what they do,'[3] he cried from the pain-drenched cross. And every prayer is begun and controlled by that word 'Abba', 'Father, dear Father', as all the prayer that he taught his followers is to be controlled.

This is not a prayer only for the secret place, in a man's own room with the door shut; it is a prayer that was prayed when Greeks on pilgrimage were crowding round for an introduction to the Galilean healer, and in the political publicity of an execution. Even if it be said that Jesus' prayer that God's will and not his own should be done was agonizingly personal, we must note that he sought the sustaining companionship of his closest friends nearby, and was grieved when their tiredness and insensitivity denied it to him. Jesus could only thus pray publicly and in desperate personal crisis because all the time he had been praying thus in the place apart and in the secret place of his own heart.

But he did pray in this way. He prayed that his own will should not be done, and that God's should be. He abandoned his autonomy, his control over his own life and destiny, and became 'resigned unto the heavenly will'. The dictionary gives these definitions of 'autonomy' when used of the individual: 'personal freedom', 'freedom of the will'. These Jesus gave up in Gethsemane. If what he did there be the best commentary we have on this petition in the Lord's Prayer, can we pray it without contradicting all that our era has taught us of the importance of human autonomy? Can it be prayed in the face of the famous letter of Dietrich Bonhoeffer to his friend Eberhard Bethge in which he looked at this human autonomy and wrote:

The attack by Christian apologetic on the adulthood of the world I consider to be in the first place pointless, in the second place ignoble, and in the third place unchristian. Pointless, because it seems to me like an attempt to put a grown-up man back into adolescence, i.e. to make him dependent on things on which he is, in fact, no longer dependent, and thrusting him into problems that are, in fact, no longer problems to him. Ignoble, because it amounts to an attempt to exploit man's weakness for purposes that are alien to him and to which he has not freely assented. Unchristian, because it confuses Christ with one particular stage in man's religiousness, i.e. with a human law.[4]

Put starkly, the question faces us, Can men be religious in this way today? Can we pray 'Thy will be done' with genuine submission, and with a real abandonment of personal freedom, of the freedom of our own wills? More even than thrusting us back into adolescence, are we not now being asked to be like little children bidden to accept that 'Father knows best'?

But when we see the best commentary on this petition in Jesus' own prayer in Gethsemane are we confronted by simple resignation, sheer submission to the will of God? Not for one moment if we think of that in terms of a folded-hands inactivity. Jesus was not only a sufferer in the Passion; he was an actor. The cross was only in one sense something that men did to Jesus; in another sense it is something in which he was most active, challenging those forces of evil in the heart of man that were bound to respond by seeking his destruction. Once we grasp this, a wholly new light is shed on the Gethsemane prayer. His natural human will – the impulse of shrinking flesh and mind – was to turn away from betrayal, agony and death. He was truly man. But to pray that God's will and not his own should be done was not to fold his hands and cease all activity; *it was to be active in pursuing this revealed will of God.*

If that be true something very important emerges for our whole understanding of praying that God's will may be done. It is that words like 'submission' and being 'resigned' subtly pervert our understanding of it. The whole tone and flavour of such words today, and the associations that they have gained, are totally misleading. We do well to abandon them entirely.

They are as misleading in the sphere of religion as they would be in the sphere of personal relationships. If a son were to say, or perhaps more likely, inwardly think, 'All right, I suppose I must submit to this plan that Dad's made,' it would not be a happy saying or thought. There would be more than a suggestion of having been treated not as a son with a mind and desires of his own, but as someone who could have his mind made up for him. He would rightly feel himself to have been treated as less than a person.

Suppose, by contrast, that a son were to say, 'Well, I haven't really seen it that way up to now, but I'm sure you've got the hang of it, and we'll do it your way,' the whole situation would be completely different. Here the son would have been taken seriously as a person. He would have freely and willingly, and quite actively, accepted his father's mind on the proposed action. He would be voluntarily committing himself to co-operation and, again it must be stressed, active co-operation.

The whole prayer is controlled by that word 'Father'. It is not only a word of address; it determines the character of all that follows. It is the Father's will, and no other, that we are talking about, and what a sensible human father asks of his grown children, even in areas where his experience is full and theirs meagre or non-existent, is not submission to his will but a free acceptance of it, and a willing commitment to doing it. Modern fathers may have wistful longings for the Victorian era in which, we understand, father's word was law, but such longings may be a foolish indulgence. We may only be asking to lose our true fatherhood. To be a father is never to be a despot. A father must face the agony of seeing his grown son reject all that seems right to the father, and embrace a course of action that he knows will be self-destructive, if that be the decision to which he freely comes. That is the way in which the greatest of Jesus' stories about the fatherhood of God begins. It begins with a son who was determined to do his own will and not his father's. And when the misery to which his choice brings him drives him home he is still treated as a son.

That, too, is a commentary on this phrase from the Lord's

Prayer. We are not asked to resign ourselves to God's will, or to submit to it; we are asked to accept it in true human freedom, and to co-operate with it to the utmost, not of our human ability, but of our willingness to receive God's power.

Our rejection, however, of concepts like submission and resignation as certainly misleading today must not lead us to minimize the costliness of what is being demanded. Our natural human resistance to the petition 'Thy will be done' does not all derive from mistaken notions of what it implies. We shrink, too, from its simple meaning. As Father Louis Evely puts it:

> Man is always frightened as soon as he realizes that he loses himself by giving himself. It is a terrible feeling, a leap in the dark... Freedom, however, does not consist essentially in being able to choose. True autonomy is the power to be able to determine for ourselves, to dispose entirely of ourselves, so as to give ourselves to others. And refusal, the fear of giving, is an inability to be available and therefore an absence of true freedom.[5]

Again we shall find the best illustration of this in personal relationships. The man who wholly disengages himself from all other human beings, never entrusting himself for a moment to the perils of commitment to another person, only remains free in a strange and perverse sense. He is free from commitments, but somehow the freedom proves to be entirely illusory. Far from being a full human being rejoicing in an unimpaired and uneroded freedom, his humanity seems to have disappeared and his freedom with it. By contrast, the man who has most fully and recklessly put his life in pawn to other people, risking his happiness (as it would seem) on the trust which he has reposed in them, even if that trust in some instances or in some part appears to have been misplaced, is most richly human, endowed with a freedom that makes the vaunted liberty of the man who 'keeps himself to himself' a pathetic sham.

Even in this sphere we often shrink back from losing ourselves, for fear of being hurt. Father Evely uses the illustration of the child caught in a house on fire whose father bids him jump into his arms. The child is more aware of the smoke, and the black hole into which he is being asked to jump.

So it is most often in faith. To pray the petition 'Thy will be done' in anything like the sense in which Jesus prayed it, meaning 'not my will but thine', demands of us a desperate leap, and one from which we shrink. It is not our essential human autonomy that is at stake here; it is our egotism. We fear the destruction of our self-hood.

Our problem with this petition is not just that it runs counter to our sense that man is called to impose his will on his environment, but that it challenges a far more dangerous force. The calling to such mastery of the environment is by no means irreligious; the book of Genesis sets forth man's appointment to dominion over the natural world. We have unjustifiably confused it with the right to reject all invitation to centre life not upon ourselves but on our Maker and his purposes. This tragic and unjustified transference of what is true in one sphere to another in which it is inapplicable has led to modern forms of the age-old sin of pride. These, equipped with the weapons which an evil use of man's environmental mastery has produced, have torn, and continue to tear, our world asunder.

Bonhoeffer's understanding of human adulthood cannot be used to buttress such egotistical evil. Remember where his letter to Bethge was written. It was the Tegel prison in Berlin. He was held there by the vileness of Nazism, and night after night the prison shook as allied bombs rained down on the German capital. A man does not exult in the unrestrained human will in such a situation of tyranny and destruction.

Far, therefore, from the petition 'Thy will be done' being one that cannot with integrity be offered by man today, the issue is whether man can find his essential salvation in praying it, whether the love of God in Christ can so constrain him that he is ready to make that leap into the dark, and abandon even the hideous and rapidly shrinking security of a world on fire with man's destruction for the Father's arms. His calling is to lose his freedom

69

by an act of commitment which will give to him a freedom that he has never known.

Every time, therefore, we pray 'Thy will be done' with meaning we are praying for deliverance from egotism, from self-will, from the ruthless determination to impose our decisions upon others. No phrase in the prayer is more demanding than this. It is the phrase that speaks of surrender, of a yielding of our wills to a greater and a better will.

It must be emphasized that it is a yielding to a personal will and not a fate. A prayer that the will of God may be done has nothing of fatalism about it. That is one further reason why it does not run counter, as we fear, to man's essential call for responsibility to master his environment. Some thirty years ago I walked round a village in what is now Bangla Desh. Some time before it had been scourged by a virulent plague of cholera. My companion, a missionary but not a medical one, had managed to secure a sufficient supply of anti-cholera vaccine to innoculate the whole population. One man, an old Muslim, who happened to be engaged in some joinery work at the missionary's house, refused. 'If it is the will of Allah that I die, then I shall', was his fatalistic attitude. 'He was the only man who did die', was my companion's quiet comment. There the will of God, as that man understood it, forbade or at least deprecated any attempt to control likely events, and to combat evils that attacked human life and happiness. Nothing could be further from the understanding of the will of God that must underlie our praying 'Thy will be done' in the Lord's prayer. It is personal will, not impersonal fate, that we pray should be done. Indeed it would be ludicrous to pray that impersonal and unavoidable fate should be 'done'; by its nature it would be inevitable, it would bear down inexorably upon the human lives that lay in its path, caring nothing for their co-operation in prayer or in anything else.

Many have found great stimulus in the writings of Simone Weil, not least because the young Jewess with an intensely secular intellectual background came with such freshness, and such vehemence, to the Christian faith when she found it. Although she would not be baptized, her ardour of spirit and fanatical discipline of will have constituted a sharp challenge to more apathetic and half-hearted Christians. But her very lack of Christian roots at times leads her to grotesque misunderstanding of the reality of Christian faith. Nowhere is this more true than when she writes of this petition:

> Everything which has happened, whatever it may be, is in accordance with the will of the almighty Father. That is implied by the notion of almighty power... We have to desire that everything that has happened should have happened, and nothing else. We have to do so, not because what has happened is good in our eyes, but because God has permitted it, and because the obedience of the course of events to God is in itself an absolute good.[6]

It may be that some sophisticated philosophical argument can be advanced to make such a position appear rationally tenable, but in the eyes of the ordinary Christian man such teaching must appear perverse to the point almost of blasphemy. Should a Christian man *desire* that Simone Weil's fellow-Jews be destroyed in Hitler's gas-chambers as she wrote, or that our atom bombs should have obliterated Hiroshima and Nagasaki? Should a Christian man desire that someone dear to him should have died of an agonizing cancer? Because these things have happened, there is no obligation whatever upon Christian men to desire that they should have happened, and to identify such events with the will of God is a relapse into pagan fatalism. It bears no relationship whatever to Jesus' prayer that the will of God should be done, that will which is the purpose of a Father who seeks nothing but good for his children.

William Temple's biographer quotes the wise words of a Bible class leader in the West Country who said as he began his class, 'Whatever we think or say, boys, let us be sure we keep clear the character of God.'[7] Simone Weil's overtowering intellect would have benefited by the control implied in that simple sentence.

Not only, however, the character of God is attacked in such

an argument, but the whole nature of man. If all that has happened is 'in accordance with the will of the heavenly Father', there is no such thing as human freedom. No meaning can be attached to the prayer – on which, strangely, Simone Weil was commenting – 'Thy will be done.' On her argument it just is done, nothing else can be done. Further, we can even say that there is no real meaning in the word 'sin'. If all that has happened is 'in accordance with the will of the heavenly Father', man is deluded in his moments of penitence. He cannot have acted contrary to the will of God, which surely is the essence of sin.

The combination of remorseless logician and wayward fanatic here provides a guide-post that would lead Christian men back to a forest of misunderstanding from which we might have hoped to have escaped for ever. At best it can only be seen as a return to the wisdom of the stoics, who in our Lord's own day, accepted the will of the gods after some such fashion. In such acceptance they found a kind of peace and serenity by not struggling against impossible odds. There is a well-known passage from one of their writers which reads: 'Do not seek to have everything that happens happen as you wish, but wish for everything to happen as it actually does happen, and your life will be serene.'

That kind of serenity, which comes from adjusting yourself to events, is in no way related to the peace which comes from accepting and co-operating with the will of God. There is perhaps only one line of Dante which has passed into our language, and it is a very simple one. It reads, 'In his will is our peace.' It is a will to be done as well as to be borne.

There is some variance amongst the scholars as to the meaning of the phrase which follows 'Thy will be done', the phrase 'on earth as it is in heaven'. Some think that it should be understood as if it read 'in heaven and earth'. The biblical writers had no word to stand for the universe in our sense, and so by mentioning heaven and earth together the same content is sought. We would then have to understand the petition as 'Thy will be done in all the world – in heaven and earth.'

The preponderance of scholarly judgment still comes down in favour of the traditional reading. What content then are we to give to 'as it is in heaven'? For Jesus, with the picture of the universe of his day, it would mean the place where, in contrast with this earth, the will of God *was* done and the result was a joyous harmony that was heaven indeed.

Understanding the phrase in that way we can readily link it to Dante's words about God's will. Where God's will is done there is peace and harmony; fighting, hatred, tension – all the things which mar human happiness and wreck our best hopes – do not invade that area of obedience. That is heaven indeed. Then our prayer becomes that we shall know here on this earth that creative, joyous harmony, that what is known in the supernatural world may be experienced here.

So to pray means that by our prayer and by our action we want to co-operate in bringing this about. Acceptance, dedication and commitment to action – not submission, resignation and emphatically not fatalism – are the essential strong notes implied in this part of the Lord's Prayer. The will of God involved for Jesus that titanic struggle with evil that took place at Golgotha, but in God's will nevertheless was his peace. While the ultimate purpose of God's will is harmony and the banishment of the things that invade our joy, commitment to the doing of God's will now may mean for us in some degree what it meant for our Master. It may involve abandonment of an uncommitted, and therefore undisturbed, existence.

That has been true again and again for the pioneers and reformers who have sought that God's will should be done in areas of social life where it was manifestly not being done. When they sought to free the slave, or to minister to the uncared-for child, or to deliver those in a harsh economic system – or when today men fight against racism or any kind of tyranny – they are trying to do the will of the heavenly Father. The resultant life for them may be quite the reverse of outwardly peaceful. It may seem as though their life before was far more peaceful. Such men would nevertheless confess that they had found their peace in God's will. It was not the stoical peace of inactivity and submission; it was the peace not of acceptance of what life brought but of sharing in God's purpose to alter the world.

Most scholars seem to agree that the phrase 'on earth as it is in heaven' does not only refer to the words that it immediately follows, 'Thy will be done.' It refers to all three of the petitions that come before it, to 'Hallowed be thy name' and 'Thy kingdom come' as well as to 'Thy will be done.' The effect of this may be seen if we set it out simply.

> Thy name be hallowed – on earth
> Thy kingdom come – on earth
> Thy will be done – on earth.

That means that having spoken to God we find ourselves looking right out across his world. It is not – and let us be sure of this – that we look up to God, and then turn round to face the world. When we turn to God we are looking at his world.

Take this seriously and it alters much of the traditional understanding of prayer and worship. For deep down in many of us there is a feeling that we are being most religious when we draw right away from the world, and try to push its intrusions out of our minds and move into a realm of calm and beauty, sweetness and light. This corresponds to something real, of course. 'Be still and know that I am God' is an abiding word. We need to stop bustling, in mind and spirit as well as body, if the scattered forces of our spirits are to be recollected, and we are to realize that we belong to the heavenly Father and that he is King 'be the earth never so unquiet'.

But there is a world of difference – perhaps just literally that – between the need for stillness and recollection and the notion that we shall find God somehow apart from his world. Gerhard Ebeling puts it arrestingly like this: 'But what if God, to whom we turn in thus turning our back on the world, has himself not his back but his face to the world?'[8] What indeed! And the Lord's Prayer suggests that his face is turned in just that direction; 'Hallowed be thy name – on earth'; 'Thy kingdom come – on earth'; 'Thy will be done – on earth.'

One of the great, and perhaps growing, tensions to be found among Christian men today is between the traditionalists and the activists. The activists in their most drastic mood would have us abandon almost everything that has come down to us as the traditional framework of the Christian life in favour of taking transforming action here on this earth – feeding the hungry, caring for the desolate and uplifting the victims of injustice. The traditionalists lament this radical breaking off from the past. They do not deny the place of care and service in the Christian role (and might stress that it has a longer history than some protagonists of a caring Christianity are prone to recognize), but they do not find them central to being a Christian. At the centre of the Christian life for them comes the life of worship and devotion. Personal prayer, the sacraments and the corporate worship of God's people are for them the heart of the Christian life, and the way of service and the search for justice are fruits of these things. It is a contrast in attitudes that has tended to become sharp in the World Council of Churches both at and since the fourth assembly of the Council held at Uppsala in 1968. It is often described in the shorthand of 'horizontal' and 'vertical' approaches to Christianity. The 'horizontal' approach believes that God will be found in the service of his needy children; the 'vertical' approach stresses that God must first serve us by pardon, cleansing and the imparting of power before we are fit to be the gracious neighbour to our fellow men.

May not some of this tension be overcome by the simple discipline of taking the Lord's Prayer seriously? The activist needs the reminder that it is God's action that we need in the world today. That, we have seen, is the real meaning of the hallowing of his name. He must see that it is God's kingdom that must come in the world, and his will that must be done. Therefore we need prayer and worship that we may centre ourselves upon that, and open mind, heart and will to give us the power to hallow the

name of God in life, to experience his kingship and to know something of his will. But no less does the traditionalist need that
reminder that Godward worship is always manward worship. To
look at God is to be looking at his world in its need of his
saving name, of his rule and of his will. True worship is never
withdrawal, or only withdrawal in the way that a man who is to
attempt a great jump runs back that he might leap the better.
True worship always brings a new vision of the world in its need
and tragedy, together with a new vision of God in his loving
fatherly purpose for just such a world. If we try to tackle the
grimness of our world with no such sustaining vision of God we
may be being heroic, but it is doubtful if we are being fully
Christian; if we lost ourselves in the beatific vision of the Divine
so as to be also lost to all concern for the doing of the will on
earth, we may be being mystical but it is doubtful if we are
being moral in any sound Christian sense.

That great missionary hero, Albert Schweitzer, gathered up his
understanding of the will of God in four simple affirmations:

To know the will of God is the greatest knowledge.
To accept the will of God is the greatest heroism.
To do the will of God is the greatest achievement.
To have the approval of God on your work is the greatest
   happiness.

To this may just be added the word of W. H. Auden which
indicates, by its use of the prayer of Jesus himself for the will of
God and not his own to be done, how central and controlling
is this petition for the whole of our praying.

Our wishes and desires – to pass an exam, to marry the person we
love, to sell our house at a good price – are involuntary and, therefore,
not in themselves prayers. They only become prayers when addressed
to a God whom we believe to know better than ourselves whether
we should be granted or denied what we ask. A petition does not
become a prayer unless it ends with the words, spoken or unspoken,
'nevertheless not as I will but as Thou wilt'.[9]

NOTES

1. T. W. Manson, *The Sayings of Jesus*, SCM Press 1949, p. 169.
2. John 12.28 (AV)
3. Luke 23.34 (AV)
4. Dietrich Bonhoeffer, *Letters and Papers from Prison* (The Enlarged Edition) ed. Eberhard Bethge, SCM Press 1961, p. 327.
5. Louis Evely, *We Dare to Say Our Father*, Herder & Herder 1965, pp. 71–72.
6. Simone Weil, *Waiting on God*, Collins Fontana 1959, p. 169.
7. F. A. Iremonger, *William Temple*, OUP 1948, p. 172.
8. Gerhard Ebeling, *The Lord's Prayer in Today's World*, SCM Press 1966, p. 76.
9. W. H. Auden, *A Certain World*, Faber 1971, p. 307.

7

OUR DAILY BREAD

Could anything seem more straightforward than the petition 'Give us this day our daily bread'? There is only one word which is not a monosyllable, and that is the very ordinary word 'daily' that only adds a 'y' to its single syllable. There is no word off-putting to our modern ears like 'heaven'; there is no word that has acquired an ill-defined religious aura like 'hallowed'; there is no word that has a legacy of twentieth-century misunderstanding like 'kingdom'. All is clear, even if there be questions about why the prayer turns so swiftly from God's name, will and rule to our basic physical needs, and why we are so suddenly plunged from the eternal world of God's character, purpose and reign to the time-bound world of our stomachs.

Since this is our natural reaction it is startling to read Dr Manson's words: '"Daily" in this verse is a guess.'[1] Any modern book on the Lord's Prayer by the time it comes to this petition takes on the aspect of a detective story which follows clues to try to solve the mystery of the Greek word which is traditionally translated 'daily'. It is the word 'epiousios'. The snag is that it is found nowhere else in Greek literature. Our reaction to this fact might well be that only a fragment of the literature that existed when the New Testament was written can have survived the ravages of time, but then that reaction is countered by the discovery that the great Christian writer Origen, who was born as early in the Christian era as AD 185, not only did not know the

78

word but could not discover anyone who did. He says, 'It seems likely that it was moulded by the evangelists.'[2]

This leaves us with the question, Why did the evangelists insert into the pattern prayer of Jesus a word apparently so exotic and unknown? Would not such an act have been plain contrary to the whole purpose of the gift of the prayer? At this point something of the fascination of the detective story again appears, for a clue arrives that has lain about for some fourteen hundred years. Towards the end of the nineteenth century discoveries were made as exciting and significant for biblical knowledge as the later discovery of the Dead Sea scrolls in the Qumran caves in 1947. These discoveries were of great quantities of papyri dating back to the early centuries of our era which, despite their fragility, had been preserved in the unique conditions of the dry heat of the Egyptian sands. The great bulk of them were of no more literary significance than the contents of our dustbins might be after we had had a good clear-out. Sets of accounts, the letters of ordinary people, wills and things of that sort were discovered. The great value of the discovery was not a rich mine of literary gold but an invaluable addition to our knowledge of that workaday Greek in which classical literature was not written but the New Testament was. The New Testament writers were engaged in communicating the good news about Jesus Christ in that day-to-day Greek in which the unearthed papyri were written.

One document that was dug up from a rubbish-heap contained the mysterious word. It was a set of accounts. To add to the baffling character of the whole business that particular piece of papyrus has by some unaccountable chance since been lost. Before the loss, however, the great archaeologist Flinders Petrie had published an account of it in 1889. The essential item reads '½ obol for epiousi'. The word is either an abbreviation, or has been broken off.[3] Another discovery elsewhere, rather romantically in the ruins of Pompeii, is of a Latin inscription on a wall which reads 'Five asses for diaria'. It has been suggested that these two words, the one Greek and the other Latin, are equivalents. It is not proved, but if they are equivalents then we know that the mysterious Greek word links with another word which means 'the coming (day)', for which our normal word is tomorrow. What is therefore referred to is daily rations issued the night before.

Both the Revised Standard Version and the New English Bible give as an alternative reading in the margin the words 'our bread for the morrow'. Two Scottish translators of different generations, Dr James Moffatt and Dr William Barclay, go the whole way and show their judgment as to the probabilities by incorporating into the text of their translations this alternative reading. Moffatt reads 'our bread for the morrow', and Barclay 'our bread for the coming day'. Dr Barclay has given his reasons for this preference in his book on the Lord's Prayer.[4]

We cannot be certain, but it seems extremely likely that this is the meaning of the mysterious word. Dr Manson comments that this would reflect the social environment of the gospels. 'The bread issued today is for consumption tomorrow, so that everyone has his food in his house overnight.' He finds illumination of this in the parable of the man knocking at midnight on the door of his more provident friend who would be certain to have his bread for the morrow in the store cupboard,[5] and even possibly in the verse 'The Lord said, Well, who is the trusty and sensible man whom his master will appoint as his steward, to manage his servants and issue their rations at the proper time?'[6] Dr Manson goes on:

This puts the petition in a new light. The disciples are God's servants, and what they ask is a sufficient provision from day to day to enable them to perform the tasks which God appoints them to do: enough today to face tomorrow's duties.[7]

The Aramaic word which Jesus must have used has been totally lost (or so it would appear unless history has stored up for us discoveries as dramatic as those of the papyri and the Dead Sea scrolls). What is clear is that when both Matthew and Luke included the best Greek equivalent that they could find for whatever word Jesus originally used, something essential was being added. Jesus taught them to pray something more than 'Give us bread today'. In a prayer in which words were so sparingly used there was this extra word which in our normal form of the prayer seems almost redundant, 'Give us this day our daily bread'. It is the only adjective in the whole of the prayer. It meant at least 'the day's ration for the day', and highly probably suggested bread for the morrow.

Let us now leave aside for a moment the added, unusual word and take special note of the placing of this petition in the prayer as a whole. We have come to the point at which the focus of the prayer changes. The first three great petitions have centred upon God – 'Hallowed be thy name, thy kingdom come, thy will be done on earth.' This does not mean that the prayers have been moving in some ethereal realm remote from this world of space and time. The phrase 'on earth' controls all three of these petitions. It is to a Father with his face towards the world that we have been praying.

But though there is now a change of focus to our needs, which seems all the sharper because the need that is first concentrated upon is the inexorable daily need of our bodies for sustaining food, there is nonetheless a logical progression. Only if we seek the hallowing of God's name, the coming of his kingdom and the doing of his will, can we rightly pray for daily provision for our physical needs. Only soldiers on the strength are entitled to draw their daily rations. A saying is attributed (probably unhistorically, but appropriately) to Napoleon, 'An army marches on its stomach.' There are no pretences in our Lord's teaching about prayer. The mystic may for a while forget his stomach when caught up into the seventh heaven, but the Christian soldier will need his grub, and does well to pray for it.

This petition is therefore illuminated as we look back to what has preceded it. In the light of the foregoing petitions it is prayer for the soldier's rations referred to in the Pompeian inscription. It is also illuminated as we look forward. This petition, and those which follow it, are all prayers for freedom. They seek freedom from hunger, from unpardoned sin, from nourished resentment and from being tested beyond strength or brought under the dominion of evil.

Some of these later freedoms that are sought seem so tremendous as to dwarf this first petition that has to do with our needs. It is an enormous thing to be freed from guilt, and to be delivered from that corroding enmity towards someone who has harmed you that can do graver harm to you than any of his actions. It is obviously a final freedom to be prevented from falling into evil's grip in the supreme tests of faith and commitment. None of these, however, form the first prayer. We move from the sublimities of the name of God, the kingdom of God and the will of God straight to freedom from hunger, not from the debasing spiritual sins of envy and resentment, not from the awesome debt we owe to God for our disobedience, but freedom from empty plates and empty bellies.

This has shocked some Christians from the first. This prayer, so understood, has been felt to be intrusive. Many early Christian writings, those of the men known as the early Fathers, have spiritualized this petition. Dr Barclay quotes the great Augustine, that it is a prayer for 'spiritual food, namely, the divine precepts which we are to think over and to put into practice each day'. Jerome producing the Vulgate, for so long the Bible of the Roman Catholic Church, introduced the phrase 'supersubstantialem panem'. You do not have to be a Latinist to recognize that this is not the sort of bread sold over the baker's counter, this supersubstantial bread. It is far more readily linked with the bread of the Holy Communion than with the bread that you put into the toaster or cut up to make a sandwich to 'keep you going'. The jump has been made from the bread by which we physically live to the bread which symbolizes the life of Christ at his Supper. It is the jump that we find in the harvest hymn:

By Thee the souls of men are fed
   With gifts of grace supernal;
Thou, who dost give us earthly bread,
   Give us the bread eternal.

The hymn writer healthily recognizes that we do need earthly bread, even if he swiftly moves on to our spiritual needs, as swiftly as he moves us from the 'burden of the day' to when we are 'to garners bright elected'.

It will never do to be more spiritual than Jesus. Surely his moving from the majestic themes of God's name, kingdom and will to our basic human need is absolutely deliberate. Let us note that it is basic need. Bread does not mean exclusively corn ground down into flour and baked into loaves. In Hebrew and Aramaic the word had become extended in its meaning when used in such a context. It meant a meal, food. There remains about it the flavour of the basic, of rations for the march not luxury for the lounge. Christ commands us to pray for essentials, not for luxuries. There is no warrant in the Lord's Prayer for asking God for things we would just like to have. If comforts and luxuries come along we must greet them with a grateful heart, taking Paul's attitude, 'I know how to live when things are prosperous.'[8] The search for them is not to form part of our prayer. If it cannot do that, are we justified in making that search a guiding-force in our lives?

There is more to this than the avoidance of the luxurious. There is the recognition that we are human beings with certain basic human needs. In Gerhard Ebeling's words, man is 'like all living things . . . a hungering thing'.[9] Man for all his proud autonomy, for all his soaring intellectual achievements in control of his world, must eat. He depends on that which is outside himself to give him the simple fuel without which all his capacity and power die. Dr Dodd writes:

The very act of taking food is a symbol of the fact that we live by that which we receive from the great universe beyond us. The Self

is dependent on the Not-self. The acknowledgment of such dependence is the beginning of religion.[10]

That last sentence points to a grave obstacle to modern man
being religious. He is irked by the thought of any such dependence, and will wriggle away from any suggestion of it. But in
this world of time we have this dependence, and to face it is
more mature and fruitful than to strive to ignore it.

It is the world of time that we are confronted by in this petition of the prayer, and we are confronted by it twice inside a
short phrase, by 'this day' and 'daily'. It is the one point when
we are reminded of that world within the prayer, and it is a
healthy reminder. No time is set for the coming of the kingdom,
but a time is set for our being fed. We need to be fed daily. We
are dependent creatures of the God to whom we are praying.
This simple human need binds us to this actual world of time
and space. We say on a country expedition, 'I have forgotten
my watch, but my stomach tells me it's lunch-time.' Time and
eating are as closely linked in our experience as they are in the
Lord's Prayer. Jesus with his 'daily' as well as 'this day' reminds
us that all our discipleship, even if it be within an eternal kingdom, here and now has to be lived out in a world of time.

C. S. Lewis finds in this a clue to how we are to expect God's
provision for our other than physical needs.

> If and when a horror turns up you will then be given Grace to help
> you. I don't think one is usually given it in advance. 'Give us this day
> our daily bread' (not an annuity for life) applies to spiritual gifts, too;
> the little *daily* support for the *daily* trial. Life has to be taken day by
> day and hour by hour.[11]

This is not a homiletic stretching of a point, or a spiritualizing
of the basic character of this petition for bread. It is the simple
recognition that all our living is time-living, and the reminder
comes in stark and simple form at the heart of the Lord's Prayer.
The natural man does not like this. He does not like living by
trust, but in security. He wants to pile up food like the man in
one of Jesus' most grim vignettes who wanted to pull down his

barns and build greater ones so that he might live independently of God's providence.[12] He wants, if asked to be Christian, to be given guarantees that when the difficult time comes plenty of heavenly aid will be stock-piled to come to his help. The words of faith are 'daily' and 'this day', and Jesus intends us to pray them in every particular while we live in this world of time.

This is clear in the light of what the scholars have discovered regarding prayer for bread in the worshipping tradition of Jesus' own people. Ernst Lohmeyer's intensive research reveals the firm change that Jesus has made.

> Wherever else in Old Testament or Jewish prayers God is asked for food and drink, either there is no suggestion of a temporal limit, or the interval is limited by a human life or even by a season.[13]

The two-fold reminder of the world of time is not just something that Jesus took over from the prayers he had been taught and heard in the synagogue. The 'daily' and 'this day' are unique: they are what Jesus himself teaches us. In the world of time we live by faith that the daily need will be met by the daily provision. It is what Newman had to discover in his growth as a disciple, that he could not expect to see 'the distant scene', but must be ready to say 'one step enough for me'. This is what living by faith and trust means. Perhaps no phrase in the whole of the prayer more sharply challenges the whole trend of today's society. That trend (too mild a word for what at times becomes almost a demonic drive) is all towards deliverance of man from dependence. Much of this is right. The squirrel as well as man makes his store for the wintry or rainy day. To seek by ingenuity, industry and prudence to be delivered from possible whims of nature is not to be godless. But to make the whole purpose of life the achievement of a total independence of providence is precisely that. It is also fruitless, because it is impossible.

Nor is only independence of providence at issue. Also involved here is our dependence on others, and their dependence upon us. In today's world anything that we can with reality describe as our daily bread is the product of complex chains of human activity stretching across the world. This note must always be sounded at any harvest festival in a city, but it is no less appropriate in a country place in any developed society. None of us lives by subsistence farming, and even by the time that Jesus' followers had taught this prayer to men who lived in Rome they would have to reflect that their daily bread came by triremes that other men manned from the granaries of north Africa and elsewhere where other men sowed and reaped. To pray for our daily bread is a form of praying for our fellowmen, and acknowledging that our life is inextricably bound up with theirs.

In a sharper form still this petition is, deeply considered, a form of praying for our fellow-man, for no man can pray only for his own bread when he stands before the Father of all men, and says 'our bread'. Every time we pray this prayer we are committed to the fight for men's freedom from hunger and committed to world development, whatever demands it may make upon our own comfort. This is no attempt to hitch a fashionable Christian band-wagon on to a New Testament prayer. It is the application of the prayer to today's world and today's opportunities. 'Is there', asked Jesus, 'a man among you who will offer his son a stone when he asks for bread? . . . how much more will your heavenly Father give good things to those who ask him !'[14] To such a Father we offer the prayer 'Give us our daily bread', and gathered round us as we pray are all the Father's children. Our prayer must be a prayer that the bread that God provides shall come to every man and not be wasted by idleness or foolishness, grabbed by greed or destroyed to satisfy avarice. We now possess the means and opportunity to see that every man, virtually anywhere in the world, receives his daily bread. The prayer has never meant that we should expect that God will feed us without effort. Dr A. M. Hunter quotes an observation that 'God feeds the sparrows, but he doesn't put the crumbs into their mouths.'[15] Plainly the prayer for our own daily bread is not prayer for provision without effort, and our prayer for the daily bread of others must involve commitment to the efforts which are appropriate to co-operation with God's creative purpose. It will mean support for many enterprises of a highly technical sort, and political action to move the wills of governments and peoples in the developed countries towards trade policies which create greater equity with the Third World, and voluntary response to the appeal of the World Council of Churches made at the fourth assembly at Uppsala in 1968 that Christians in the richer nations should tax themselves 1% of their 'take-home pay' in support of development projects.

All these actions are possible to us, and their possibility may be thought to render them obligatory for all who would pray 'Give us this day our daily bread' with full intention and the widest meaning. The simplest man in the least complicated situation would not expect to pray thus for his own daily bread without digging, sowing and reaping: man today in all the complexity of his world must not expect to pray it without commitment to sophisticated enterprises that he may be tempted to consider far from the Galilean simplicity of the original prayer. Man today is not in Galilee, and his situation is not simple. He has no right whatever to escape from the challenge of the prayer by such pious evasions. As John Parkinson has said, 'When we pray "Give us this day our daily bread", we are asking God to change men's hearts,'[16] but one of the hearts to be changed is our own, and the change of heart must show itself in commitment to some very down-to-earth but also high-powered action.

This is not a prayer to be spiritualized, as we have seen, or to have the sharp edge of it smoothed away. It is a prayer about bread, about the food that keeps me and my brother alive, the food that I will not get if my brother fails me and that he will not get if I fail him. When a Christian man who has never heard of that mysterious word 'epiousios' (or the Egyptian papyrus, or the Pompeian inscription, or what the early Fathers thought) kneels down by his bed, or joins with his local congregation, and prays

'Give us this day our daily bread', meaning his daily ration of food to be a faithful servant of God that day or week out in the world, he is praying as Jesus taught him. The more aware he is of his brother when he prays the prayer – and Jesus warned us always to be aware of our brother when we turned to worship – the richer will his prayer be.

There remains the possibility that there may be a deeper symbolism here which does not deny the prayer for ordinary bread but enriches it. For that same Christian man as he has read the gospels and thought about the words of Jesus will have been struck by how they are always eating and talking about eating. There are two separate occasions recorded of the miraculous feeding of multitudes. You have a story about people arguing heatedly about where they should be placed at a high-class dinner, and another about the reactions of people who had found better things to do when the time to fulfil their acceptance of a supper invitation turned up. There is another story about a man with his friends wining and dining on the best while a beggar made do with the crusts they had wiped their hands on and hurled through the window-space. You have accusations that Jesus was always attending the wrong people's dinners, and suggestions from his enemies that he was too fond of his food. When it came to the crisis of his life it was a carefully planned supper party with his friends which he invested with profound and mysterious meaning.

Calling these things to mind, that praying Christian would recognize the truth of Ernst Lohmeyer's words, based on a thorough and careful examination of all of which the ordinary Christian may only have a general impression:

... while in the Old Testament there are many vivid pictures which paint the glory of the final kingdom, in the words of Jesus there is only one, which is drawn many times, the picture of the marriage feast or the king's feast, of eating and drinking or reclining at table with the patriarchs, in Abraham's bosom, and the pictures of harvest or sowing only serve to show the great context in which 'our bread' is situated.

One might almost say that from this point of view to pray for the coming of the kingdom and to pray 'Give us our bread today' amounted to the same thing.[17]

The words 'the great context' deserve to be given full weight, for the context is that for Jesus the single symbol he used of the final consummation of the kingdom – when it had come and the will of the heavenly Father was being perfectly done – was eating, the common sign of fellowship and joy. To this now we must add the high probability (which we saw at the beginning of this chapter) that there is a hint of the future in the mysterious word that we translate as 'daily' bread. It might more accurately mean 'tomorrow's bread'. There is a hint and foretaste of the future about it, an eating of 'tomorrow's bread today'; it is a foretaste of that future when God's name is fully hallowed, the kingdom has come, and the will is being done so that men neither grab nor starve.

The Quakers keep no sacraments. They affirm that any meal eaten in the right spirit can be sacramental, can in fact be the Lord's Supper with Jesus as the invisible host. This may be too high a doctrine for many of us, and those of us who treasure the Holy Communion as an appointed sacrament may regret what they deny. We can nonetheless strongly welcome what they are affirming. There is a word of Christ in their emphasis. Perhaps the Early Fathers were only partly wrong when they often linked this phrase with the Holy Communion. They were wrong in what they excluded. When they so spiritualized this prayer that it had nothing to do with bread, food for people's ordinary meal-tables, for those whose hungry stomachs were telling them that supper-time had come, they distorted and obscured the healthy realism of our Lord. Even worse, they removed a vast range of obligation from Christian men. If you need only be concerned about the availability of the sacrament for your brother and not whether he is going to get a daily square meal your conscience has to carry a far lighter burden. Possibly even worse still, and wholly contrary to biblical insights, they took away the relevance of the Lord's Prayer to the created world. Dietrich Bonhoeffer commented on this petition: 'It is not God's will that his creation should be despised.'[18] Once you start despising God's creation (and that is what you are doing when you are ashamed of the plain meaning of this petition), you have abandoned the God of the Bible for some divinity of your own devising.

They could still have been right in what they positively suggested. To link this prayer with the Lord's Supper does illuminate it. At that supper it is bread, real bread, that is used, and that supper was to be a foretaste for the followers of Jesus of the kingdom of God coming in all its fulness, with the will of God perfectly done, and men sitting down in unimpeded and fully open fellowship with one another. They were to have bread that day with the taste in it of a glorious tomorrow. 'Give us this day tomorrow's bread' – that may be part of what the Master taught, that Master on whose lips feasting was the incomparable illustration of the divine promise for the future.

On one thing all modern writers on the Lord's Prayer seem totally agreed, that is, that it is eschatological through and through in all its parts. That daunting word means that it refers to the 'eschaton' all the way through, and the 'eschaton' is the end, the consummation. That does not mean, as we have already seen, that this removes the prayer from present and immediate relevance. It means that that relevance is always seen most fully when we recognize that it is a prayer that takes the longest conceivable perspective. It is a prayer for now because it is a prayer for the most final 'then'.

So we pray 'Give us this day our daily bread' in simplicity with its most obvious and personal intention. But, thinking of the whole range of Jesus' teaching and his giving of the bread at the last to his followers whom he had taught thus to pray, we can also pray it with ever deepening intention, that God's daily provision for our needs may be the symbol and reminder of the promises of God, and of a future that is in his hands. Our daily ration, yes, but with something of the flavour of to-morrow's bread, a foretaste of the great fulfilment.

NOTES

1. T. W. Manson, *The Sayings of Jesus*, SCM Press 1949, p. 169.

2. See A. C. Deane, *The Lord's Prayer*, Hodder & Stoughton 1938, p. 73.

3. C. F. Evans, *The Lord's Prayer*, SPCK 1963, p. 48.

4. William Barclay, *The Plain Man Looks at the Lord's Prayer*, Collins Fontana 1964, pp. 91–92.

5. Luke 11.5 ff.

6. Luke 12.42 (NEB)

7. Manson, op. cit., p. 169.

8. Phil. 4.12 (J. B. Phillips' translation).

9. Gerhard Ebeling, *The Lord's Prayer in Today's World*, SCM Press 1966, p. 91.

10. C. H. Dodd in *Christian Worship* ed. Nathaniel Micklem, OUP 1936, p. 80.

11. *Letters of C. S. Lewis* ed. W. H. Lewis, Geoffrey Bles 1966, p. 250.

12. Luke 12.18.

13. Ernst Lohmeyer, *The Lord's Prayer*, Collins 1965, p. 139.

14. Matt. 7.9 (NEB)

15. A. M. Hunter, *Design for Life*, SCM Press, rev. ed. 1965, p. 75.

16. John Parkinson, *Kingdom Come*, Geoffrey Bles 1970, p. 68.

17. Lohmeyer, op. cit., p. 148.

18. Dietrich Bonhoeffer, *The Cost of Discipleship*, SCM Press 1948, p. 144.

8

FORGIVE US

When I was a young theological student for the Presbyterian ministry in England I had the opportunity of gaining my first holiday in Scotland by taking Sunday duty at a church midway between Glasgow and Edinburgh. Fortunately, in England I had a Scottish minister who gave me a timely warning or two. Both related to the Lord's Prayer. I was not to be surprised if when I introduced it no one joined with me in saying it. (It was a useful warning, for no one did and this would have startled me: the prejudice even in the later thirties against praying in 'forms' was still strong north of the Border.) And whatever I did I was to say 'debts' and 'debtors' in the prayer, and not 'trespasses' and 'trespass'. Otherwise I would be dismissed as quite irredeemably 'English'.

It was a reminder that the customary form in England derived, not (as in Scotland) from the Authorized Version of the Bible, but from an earlier tradition, the work of Tyndale, Rogers and Coverdale, that was given abiding currency through its incorporation in the Book of Common Prayer. The non-liturgical churches in England have followed the Church of England in using the older and earlier form. Scotland, however, in taking the Authorized Version form of 'debts' and 'debtors' has chosen the more accurate if less euphonious part. It is the better translation even if it takes away the verbal wit and felicity of a placard I saw on the building site of a church being constructed on the outskirts of New Delhi, which read 'Trespassers will be forgiven'.

The Aramaic word that Jesus used did not stand for what we today would mean by trespasses. It stood for debts or sins. Luke in his version of the Lord's Prayer used the Greek word for sins. What we have here is not a difference of meaning but a variation in translation of a word which carried both senses. What is interesting is not the variation, but the fact that it was possible for both words to be used with accuracy, for the word Jesus used bore this two-fold meaning. Our sins are our debts to God in the sense that we have failed to pay to God what we owe to him.

Here we enter a difficult area in the use of the Lord's Prayer today in a fresh sense. It is not difficult to understand, as 'hallowed be thy name' might be considered to be. It is not even difficult in the way 'thy will be done' might be, although this difficulty is a related one. That we saw to raise questions for man's sense of autonomy, his unwillingness to have his independence as a mature being invaded by genuinely praying that not his will should be done but that of another, even if that other be God. To praying that prayer there could be a resistance related to the modern man's sense of control over his life and his world.

The difficulty with 'Forgive us our debts (or sins)' is a different one. It is one of feeling as much as of thought. Here are two petitions that tumble one after the other, the one to do with bread and the other with forgiveness. But one deals with an actual necessity that all must recognize, the other only with a religious need. No one can doubt that he needs bread (even if he does not see what God has to do with the provision of it). If we do not get the physical necessities of life it stops. But do we in the same essential sense need pardon? For health and even continued existence we must have bread; it is a hunger from which no man can escape. By contrast is the hunger for forgiveness only artificially induced in the personalities of those who have been religiously indoctrinated?

That is to put it the harsh way, the way that denies reality to faith in God; but put the same point in a less slanted way and we are near the answer. We only hunger for forgiveness if we have prayed with sincerity the part of the prayer that precedes the petition for pardon. If we have said 'Our Father' and meant it, if with some real content we have wanted to see the name of God hallowed in the world, and his kingdom come among men, and his will done on earth, then we have become aware that we have not lived as children of the Father, nor treated others as our brothers, nor hallowed the name of the Holy Father by the quality of our living, not sought first his kingdom and his justice, and have said all too often 'Not thy will but mine be done.' It is as simple as that. It is in the degree that we have become 'religiously indoctrinated', as irreligious men will put it, or in the degree that we have come to a living faith in the Holy Father revealed in Jesus of Nazareth, as the Christian man will choose to put it, that we hunger for pardon.

It is at the point at which we have through prayer been brought into living fellowship with the Holy Father that we know that we are in debt, and that there is only one thing that we can ask about that debt. The one thing we can ask is that God will write it off, forgive us and treat us as if we were not debtors at all. It may be objected that that is not treating the word 'debt' as a synonym for 'sin' with adequate seriousness. A debt can be paid back, however slowly. But supposing a naval commander wrecked his aircraft carrier by culpable negligence, how seriously would we take his assurance to the Board of Admiralty, 'I'll pay you for it: I'll pay you what I owe'? It could yet be wildly possible if by chance he owned a few oil-wells; but the debt we owe to God is quite literally unpayable since we have no possessions in reserve like that. All that we have and all that we are we owe to him. It has all been given us for the doing of his will. We have no extra to pay in the future for what we owe for the past. We owe the Father all our loyalty: we cannot say, 'I'll serve you better than I am really obliged to do to make up for all that I've done wrong.'

Take the word 'Father' seriously, and take the word 'debt'

seriously, and we are straightaway ushered into the area of grace. Our Father can only forgive us; he cannot space out the repayments. And Jesus tells us to pray for just that action by God, a writing off of the clinging past such as will enable us to be as fresh and whole in spirit as the gift of our daily bread will make us in body. Jesus taught us so to pray because he knew it to be the purpose of his Father and ours to give us just that. 'Forgive us our debts' is the prayer for a new beginning.

The honest answer we are compelled to give to the modern man's questioning of the hunger for pardon is that it is a hunger awakened in the heart of the man brought into living contact with the Holy Father. But once we say 'Forgive us our debts' is the prayer for a new beginning, we reveal a universal hunger, by no means confined to the man of faith. The craving for a new beginning has a universality and a vehemence that can readily be equated with the hunger of the body for food. That craving may be all too little related to any sense of personal moral responsibility, any sense of sin, as the man of faith would put it; but there is a general sense that life has gone awry. Man today may query the whole concept of divine forgiveness, but he does not question the desirability of a new beginning. He may despair of it, and many of the most influential writers of our day do precisely that, but the point of divergence is not that the religious man is dissatisfied with his world and the man of no religion is pleased with it. The point of divergence is that the man of faith believes that there can be a new beginning, and the man of no faith rejects the possibility. The man of faith believes that he can pray, 'Father ... forgive us our debts', and find it to be an answered prayer.

If the first part of this petition worries the man of today who rejects the whole idea of divine pardon, it is the second half which has troubled many deeply religious men. This is the only petition in the Lord's Prayer that has a condition attached to it. 'As we forgive our debtors' suggests that the grace of God in pardon is conditioned by our own activity, or the lack of it. It was this severe condition that caused St Augustine to call this 'the terrible petition'.

Many commentators wrestle with this issue with only too obvious discomfort, and the more evangelical their convictions the more profound their discomfort becomes. The heart of evangelical doctrine is that Christ on his cross, in the words of the liturgy, 'made there (by his one oblation of himself once offered) a full, perfect, and sufficient sacrifice, oblation and satisfaction, for the sins of the whole world'. The very piling up of adjectives and nouns is intended to exclude the faintest qualification of the one ground of God's pardon. Do we then amazingly find in the Lord's Prayer, of all places, the suggestion that our pardon was not wholly won for us by Christ, but is in fact something which in a measure we earn by our being forgiving towards others?

It seems quite clear that Jesus was not dealing with all this at all. He was speaking about something very down-to-earth which has a great deal to do with our praying. He was telling us that we cannot *experience* forgiveness unless we are forgiving. General Oglethorpe, to whom the young John Wesley was chaplain in the colony of Georgia, once said to his chaplain with great pride, 'I never forgive.' Wesley replied, 'Then I hope, sir, you never sin.' That is the issue in a nutshell, for the unforgiving man cannot really believe in forgiveness.

It is not only in regard to forgiveness that this principle operates. Who has not met mean and cynical men who cannot believe in generosity? Tell them of some such act, some gift of simple and splendid generosity, and their immediate reaction is, 'What does he expect to get out of it? There's more to this than meets the eye.' They will plunge after any explanation, no matter how far-fetched, save that there had been a genuine act of warm generosity. Since they cannot be generous themselves, and their own springs of generous feeling have become silted up with selfishness, they must deny the reality of generosity. It has no meaning for them, and so it logically follows that what looks like disinterested generosity can only be that in appearance. There is no such thing, only self-interest in many subtle disguises.

It is like that with forgiveness. That which we do not practise, even in the most feeble way, ceases to have reality for us. More than that, if like General Oglethorpe you pride yourself on being unforgiving, you can hardly expect God to be less exalted in his behaviour. If being unforgiving is a virtue, then God must possess it. You are wise then, as Wesley said, never to sin.

Dag Hammarskjöld has expressed the issue thus:

'To forgive oneself' – ? No, that doesn't work: we have to *be forgiven*. But we can only believe this is possible if we ourselves can forgive.[1]

This is no playing with words. It is how human nature works, and Jesus knew what was in man. A man must believe in forgiveness if he is to have the ability to receive the gift that God always wants to give him. You do not believe in forgiveness if, like General Oglethorpe, you make a virtue of not practising it.

We must not misunderstand the word 'as' in the most familiar version of the Lord's Prayer, 'Forgive us our trespasses, as we forgive them that trespass against us.' It does not carry the suggestion 'in the degree that', so that the sluice-gates of God's mercy are opened or closed according to the few creaky turns by which we have been prepared to open our hearts in forgiveness of others. (Luke's version, 'For we ourselves forgive every one that is indebted to us', may be seen as refuting any such suggestion.) It means that we have made what little preparation we can make to receive God's gift. We have shown, even if in a meagre way, that we do believe in forgiveness.

Even, however, to put it like this may mislead us. It suggests a wrong succession of events, whereby we do some forgiving and then pray to be forgiven by God. A better time sequence is suggested by our Lord's words about coming to make the worshipping gift, realizing that there is something wrong between you and your brother, going to put it right, and then resuming worship.[2] Portia, in *The Merchant of Venice*, points to the power of this petition in the Lord's Prayer to *teach* forgiveness:

> *We do pray for mercy,*
> *And that same prayer doth teach us all to render*
> *The deeds of mercy.*

A Shakespearean scholar,[3] commenting on these lines, points to the only parallel to the petition and suggests that they could therefore be meaningful even to the non-Christian Shylock to whom they are addressed. It is found in the book of Ecclesiasticus 28.2–5.

> Forgive thy neighbour the hurt that he hath done thee; and then thy sins shall be pardoned when thou prayest. Man cherisheth anger against man; and doth he seek healing from the Lord? Upon a man like himself he hath no mercy; and doth he make supplication for his own sins? He being himself flesh nourisheth wrath: who shall make atonement for his sins?

But Dr Manson comments on this:

> But generally the Jewish insistence is on the duty of the offender to seek forgiveness of the injured party; that of Jesus on the duty of the injured party to offer forgiveness. Jesus would not, we may presume, have condemned the Jewish doctrine: nor would the Pharisees perhaps have condemned that of Jesus. It is a matter of emphasis; and it is the characteristic teaching of Jesus that is emphasised in this petition.[4]

Thus our petition does not read, 'Forgive us the wrong that we have done, as we have sought forgiveness from those we have wronged.' It is our business to forgive those who have wronged us. There has to be some reflection of the free grace of God in our own lives if we are to be true children of our Father who is in heaven.

Again Jesus knew what was in man. We are far more conscious of the debts that we are owed than the debts we owe. Let someone borrow a pound note from me and the loan is written ineffaceably on the tablets of my memory; but the fact that I have borrowed a pound note has a fascinating power to slip through the many interstices of that all-too-fallible organ. And being what we are, we are far more conscious of the wrongs that have been done to us than we are of the wrongs that we have done. Let our sensitive feelings be hurt, and how incessantly they smart! But let us trample on the feelings of others, and we are hardly aware that there has been anything but pavement under our feet. Did Jesus ask us to be forgiving towards others, rather than stress our duty of asking the forgiveness of others, because he knew that this was a far more real test of how much we believe in forgiveness?

Just as at many points the life of Jesus himself gives us the best commentary we can have on the various petitions of the Lord's Prayer, so we find in one of his most dramatic stories a full commentary on the part of the prayer we are now considering. It is the parable of the unmerciful servant.[5] In the Authorized Version its conclusion even echoes the familiar wording of the Lord's Prayer, 'So likewise shall my heavenly Father do also unto you, if ye from your hearts forgive not every one his brother their trespasses.'

The situation from which the story sprang, according to Matthew, was Peter's question about how often he must forgive and his characteristic offer to forgive his brother seven times. It was characteristic because there was an element of showing-off in it. Rabbis taught that you should forgive three times. Peter was displaying his magnanimity. Then Jesus shatters him by saying that he ought to forgive seventy times seven, in effect, until he had lost count. Exactly, because for Jesus forgiveness had to be taken out of the realm of the legal, the calculated. The forgiving spirit has nothing to do with arithmetic and has a splendid inability to keep accounts.

Then comes the story of the king and one of his governors, who owes an unimaginable amount. The king, ignoring the futile and meaningless offer by the man, given time, to pay it back, freely forgives him. Then at the very moment when the forgiven man comes out of the king's presence, with that incredible pardon still ringing in his ears, he takes a man who owes him a pound or two by the throat, and has him thrown into jail until he has paid the last penny. That could be years, since a man in jail was not earning anything.

His colleagues' horror at this appalling action causes him to be brought back to the king and a sterner judgment, 'You, scoundrel, weren't you bound to show your fellow-servant the same pity as I showed to you?'

It is plain commentary on 'Forgive us our debts, as we forgive our debtors'. There is no suggestion here that the governor earned his forgiveness by the king. It is freely given: it is sheer grace. But if forgiveness is genuinely experienced large consequences flow from it. The answer to Peter's question was that forgiveness is not accountancy, it is gratitude. Peter did not want God to ration his pardon to him, so why did he think it a matter for self-congratulation that he was ready to outstrip the rabbis' precept and go as far as to forgive an offending brother seven times? God does that for you every hour of the day, for the twinge of bitter resentment, the moment of offended pride, the lascivious thought, the facile self-deception. Think of that, and let warm gratitude and not cold arithmetic be the driving force of your forgiveness.

To Jesus the unforgiving spirit in men with any knowledge and experience of the merciful Father was as incredible and morally horrifying as the action of that governor in taking his humbler colleague by the throat as he came out of the audience chamber with his own fantastic debt forgiven him.

It is appalling to recognize that the Christian church in its organized life has in large measure refused to learn this plain lesson. It may be true that the moral discipline that it has sought to exercise amongst its members – from the earliest days, see the letters of Paul – was an aspect of love. There is no warrant in the gospels for a faith without moral demand. Some of the talk today about the need for the church to be only an 'accepting society' ignores this. The fact remains that the church's life down the centuries has often been marked by a judging, moralizing attitude that suggests something quite other than a society of forgiven men, of people who have just come out of the audience chamber with an unrepayable debt totally and freely written off.

The story also gives us the profound answer to why God cannot forgive us our debts if we remain unwilling to forgive those who have offended us. What that king did was to restore the governor to intimacy and trust; he wiped out the past and gave him the chance to start a new life in which the relationship with his king was unmarred. More than that, the king had shown himself as one who rose above the current notions of despotic rule to show a wonderful spirit of pity and compassion. This tells us the kind of man he was. When the governor went out and treated his humbler colleague so vilely he showed that he was unfit and unable to have an intimate relationship with a king of such a spirit.

'Forgiveness means restoration to intimacy,' as William Temple once said. By being unforgiving you show that you do not want to be intimate with a forgiving Father, and by this you reject forgiveness. Fellowship with a forgiving God is only possible for those who delight in mercy.

Not in doctrinal questionings about how we relate 'as we forgive them that trespass against us' to sound evangelical teaching, but in this parable shall we find illumination on the petition for pardon in the Lord's Prayer. In that story Jesus put two things right up against one another, a man's complacent acceptance of vast forgiveness for himself, and a total inability even to conceive the idea of forgiveness on a petty matter for another. It is the Lord's Prayer turned upside down.

This 'terrible petition', terrible because it has the condition attached to it, takes us to the heart of the gospel. Grace can never be stagnant, but must always be flowing. It is a constant theme of Jesus' ministry. He is startled at the failure of most of the healed lepers to return to give thanks, surprised at the indignation of the disciples about the outpouring of the ointment, for it was natural that one who had been forgiven much should love much, certain that the way of forgiveness was one of the chief routes to happiness; 'Blessed are the merciful: for they shall obtain mercy.'[6] Gratitude for grace shown in a forgiving spirit was so central to a right relationship with the heavenly Father that he varied the pattern of his prayer to make the point plain. The essential overspill from praying to living is made explicit here, but left implicit elsewhere. It is as though Jesus is determined that at this central point there must be no doubt that when a man prays for forgiveness he is making a commitment to the way of forgiveness. It is indeed 'the terrible petition'.

NOTES

1. Dag Hammarskjöld, *Markings*, Faber 1964, p. 133.
2. Matt. 5.23–24.
3. Richmond Noble, *Shakespeare's Biblical Knowledge*, SPCK 1935, pp. 167–168.
4. T. W. Manson, *The Sayings of Jesus*, SCM Press 1949, p. 170.
5. Matt. 18.23–35.
6. Matt. 5.7 (AV)

9

TEMPTATION AND THE TEST

Nowhere does familiarity more mask the strangeness of what we are saying than in the petition 'Lead us not into temptation.' We say it readily because we were taught it early in life, and it has the authority of being the Lord's Prayer. But once we stop to think about it, as we are bound to do in such a study as this, the mind bristles with all kinds of questions.

The first, and most obvious, is, Whoever would think that God would lead us into temptation? And this on two plain grounds. One is that the God revealed to us not only by Jesus but by the Old Testament prophet is a God of holiness, and a holiness not of mysterious and almost magical taboo but of righteousness beyond our highest conceiving. Our understanding of holiness, as revealed when we say of a saintly man, 'He is a holy man', meaning a man of outstanding goodness, derives from that revelation of the nature of God in the Bible. It is inconceivable that the leading of such a God should be other than in the paths of righteousness.

The other plain ground relates to this. This study of the Lord's Prayer has stressed that the way in which God is addressed controls the whole prayer. It is a prayer to 'Our Father', and though the divine Fatherhood must totally soar above earthly conceptions of fatherhood that is the only way in which it must differ from them. It must be infinitely higher than the best of human fatherhood that we know. It certainly must not be lower.

But what good, what even rational, human father would need

a request from his children, 'Don't give us sticks of dynamite to play with; don't lead us into deep water when we can't swim; don't leave bottles of poisonous weed-killer about the place'? No father worthy of the name would for a moment contemplate action that would make it easy for his children to injure themselves. Why then should the God whom we are being taught to pray to as Father be thought for one moment to need so strange a plea?

That is one question, and the most obvious one. But, oddly, if we think for a moment longer a quite contrary one comes into our minds. It is, Is it right to pray for the avoidance of temptation? To take the analogy just used, it may be absurd and even grotesque for a father to need a plea not to tempt his children with the means of injury or self-destruction, but it is also quite wrong for a father to keep his children back from all challenges, even though, of course, those challenges would need to be within their capacity to face. A father who kept his children away from all possibility of temptation, sheltered them from the dirt and grit of life so that temptation could not get near them (if that were possible), would be a bad father. He would be, even if from good intentions, deliberately preventing the maturity and responsibility of his children. So, in a quite different sense, is there not something awry in this later petition in the Lord's Prayer?

Is it not, in fact, perilously near to a prayer not to live? If a man is truly to live, and have the possibility of growing and deepening in maturity, can he be delivered from harsh moral choices? Are these not the very occasion and opportunity of our showing the reality of our commitment to the service of God, and therefore the genuineness of our prayer that his kingdom should come, and his will should be done? It could be seen as a prayer to be delivered from all moral adventure. Marcus Dods went as far as to say, 'Temptation is our only opportunity for growth – a very commonplace truth, but lying at the root of our whole condition in this world.'[1] So seen, this petition would be one to be allowed to play safe; then it would be at odds with so much else in Jesus' teaching where the man who takes the plunge is so much admired, the man who puts his hand to the plough and does not look back, or swiftly sells a lifetime's collection to gain the one priceless pearl. Jesus' preference for the adventurer is even more clear in his choice of his chief disciple, the man he called the Rock. Peter was above all a man who ran into temptation. Even his confession of Jesus as the Christ led him there, for a moment later he is contradicting Jesus in his understanding of what being Messiah meant. His attempt to walk to Jesus on the water was a running into temptation, when faith began to fail and fear took over. Most of all, by following the captive Jesus into the courtyard of the High Priest he marched into temptation. But it was a man of this character whom Jesus chose for this central role among his followers. It is not easy to read this into any prayer to avoid the occasions of temptation.

Thus you have two questions that are in a measure contradictory. A third can be added to them. It is again a simple one. Is it possible to think of temptation as something that we need to be led into? No one, God or man, necessarily leads us into temptation. It is not some distant ground, like a dangerous swamp or quicksand, that we shall readily avoid if only someone does not lead us in that direction: it seems, in the experience of most of us, the ground under our feet, and the air we breathe. It is the images that assail our eyes, the minute-by-minute assaults on our senses from without, and the hammering that even our memories can give us from within. *Leading* into temptation? Why, we have only to get on to an Underground escalator, or to turn over the pages of a colour supplement, to be battered by advertisements based on lust. We have only to turn on the commercial channel of television to have envy-tipped darts thudding into our consciousness. The old Adam in us, without benefit of external stimuli, tempts us to sloth and apathy, while the people we meet may tempt us towards ill-temper, or arrogance, or contempt.

Most emphatically temptation is no distant swamp towards which we must be led. It *is* the ground under our feet, the air we breathe, the people we meet, the whole complex of desires and emotions and memories that is bundled together to form the beings that we are.

What then are the answers to these questions which arise as we ponder this strange petition? Is the first one true, that it degrades the true understanding of God to picture him needing us to plead with him not to lead us into temptation? We could buttress our questioning at this point by noting that it is the only petition in the whole prayer which is in the negative form, that introduces the word 'not'. All other petitions ask for something to be done, the name to be hallowed, the kingdom to come, the will to be done, the bread given and forgiveness imparted. Only at this point are we bidden to ask for something not to happen. Does this suggest that the words have been sadly changed, that Jesus, everywhere in the gospels portrayed as commanding positive actions instead of announcing negative prohibitions, has somehow had words attributed to him which have no warrant in anything that he actually said?

The scholar who has written the most exhaustive modern study of the Lord's Prayer, Ernst Lohmeyer, says that there are no significant variations at this point amongst the manuscripts of Matthew and Luke that we have.[2] While this is true of the early manuscripts, it is certainly significant that the wording is very varied in later versions. One of the early Fathers, Dionysius of Alexandria, writing in the third century, adds an interpretative comment, 'That means, let us not fall into temptation.' There is evidence, too, that much earlier Christians in Asia Minor used the petition in the form, 'And let us not be brought into temptation.' It appears to be the form in which they knew this petition as early as towards the end of the century in which Jesus lived on earth.

Therefore the problem we have posed is not one that has just arisen in the modern era. It was a problem from the earliest days.

Christians felt some difficulty with the thought the words of Matthew and Luke implied, and there was in consequence a movement towards a certain interpretation of them. Even before the canon of the New Testament was closed there was fairly substantial evidence of this, if we interpret one verse in the Letter of James as dealing with this issue, as it appears to do. James wrote firmly, 'No one under trial or temptation should say "I am being tempted by God"; for God is untouched by evil, and does not himself tempt anyone.'[3] It can scarcely be put more emphatically and plainly than that. It certainly looks as though a common misunderstanding is being given its necessary correction. (We may note in passing that the re-interpretation of the words in this way has become the way in which French-speaking people say this petition, for we could translate their form as 'And do not let us succumb to temptation.')

There still remains a question in this area. It is, Was the early church justified in making that kind of interpretation? It is a reasonable principle of all textual criticism in any literature to prefer the hard reading to the easy one. A reading which presents a problem is far more likely to be smoothed away by a scribe or copyist than a hard reading is likely to be introduced by one. Here you have two gospels enjoying originally separate circulation, and copied out by different scribes, and the evidence of the early manuscripts is unanimous for the reading that creates the difficulties. Is this an unexpected thought of Jesus, with which we ought to grapple, however hard the difficulties? Had those early Christians who put an interpretative gloss on these strong words any warrant for doing so?

One answer to this would be that if the words were leading to a distorted and false picture of God it was wholly right that this interpretation should be given. Particular phrases of the gospels must always be interpreted by the whole understanding of the character of God that Jesus revealed. But, perhaps more important, it has now become clear that this is the right interpretation, for this would be the sense in which Jesus understood these words, and in which they would have been taken by the first disciples, to whom they were imparted.

The difficulty only arose when these words came to be used by those who did not, as all the first disciples did, stand in the Jewish worshipping tradition. In his article 'The Lord's Prayer in Recent Research'[4] Professor Joachim Jeremias points to an ancient Jewish evening prayer which Jesus could very well have known. Certainly it represents a way in which it was natural for the thought to be expressed devotionally in his day. The relevant portion of the prayer (which is also repeated in a morning prayer) reads as follows:

> Lead my foot not into the power of sin,
> And bring me not into the power of iniquity,
> And not into the power of temptation,
> And not into the power of anything shameful.

To put in simpler terms Professor Jeremias' comment which follows, we may say that the object of the prayer is not to plead with God not to do these things, but to plead with him not to permit them to happen. It is prayer that we do not fall under the power of sin, iniquity, temptation and things shameful. It is not prayer that we be not tempted, but that we do not fall into the pit that temptation has dug and towards which it so beguilingly entices us.

The early interpretations, therefore, were not a distortion of Jesus' words but an accurate rendering of their sense. When we say the Lord's Prayer we must understand the petition as 'Do not let us succumb to temptation.'

What then about our second question which was, Do we do well to pray to be delivered from temptation? If the Jewish prayer to which Professor Jeremias refers gives some of the flavour of the petition in the Lord's Prayer then there is at least an element in its asking God not to permit us to be led into temptation. Is not this in Dr Floyd Filson's telling phrase, to 'contradict life, which inevitably involves choices between good and evil, and so brings us into temptation'? He adds, 'We cannot ask God to keep us from life's struggles and decisions.'[5]

Once again we must interpret the prayer by the life of Jesus. If Jesus had personally prayed to be delivered from temptation it was an unanswered prayer. His ministry begins with the massive and succcessive temptations in the wilderness across Jordan, temptations which went piercingly to the heart of his mission to men. Different ways of gaining the allegiance of men and women plucked at his heart and mind with a terrible force. The close of his life in the flesh brought temptation in even more anguished form, the temptation to turn away from the agony and death to which his obedience across Jordan had now led him. When temptation thus moulded the life and ministry of our Master how can he bid us pray to avoid it?

To this three things can briefly be said. One is that while temptation may be in one sense the stuff of life, if life be seen as a succession of moral choices, that does not mean that we can play with it. Montaigne remarked that when he was playing with his cat he was never quite sure that his cat was not playing with him. When we are playing with temptation we can be very sure that temptation is playing with us. In this aspect the petition has the sense 'Let us not run into temptation with foolish self-confidence.' It is extraordinarily easy to do just that. We are quite sure that we can play with temptation, and that we can determine what we do with it. All human experience should teach us otherwise. Few men who fall into appalling crimes set out to commit them, for few men say, 'Evil be thou my good.' They begin by playing with temptation. And our more wretched moral failures rarely come from deliberate intent. They come from a delicate, and – as we thought – controlled, walk into the field of temptation. We do well, in the simplest terms, to pray 'Don't let us go into temptation.' Let not the fact that we can boldly call God Father give us exalted ideas of our own moral capacity. If we humbly pray not to be tempted, but then life presents us with an inevitable moral choice between good and evil, we can rightly expect the moral power to be given us to make the right choice. We cannot expect God to armour us for situations into which he has not bidden us go.

It is highly improbable that Jesus was here referring to that kind of temptation which is built into living, the inevitable moral choice between good and evil. When we face the moral choices which afford us the opportunity of growing in character we are more aware of the good that is challenging us to respond, than the evil or less good which is the alternative. Thus a man who faces the challenge to give up the securities, affections and comforts of home to tackle a tough piece of service across the world is facing that positive challenge. He is not really facing the temptation to be unresponsive and stay at home. That temptation may be there by implication, but the element of potentiality for growth in the situation is the positive challenge, not the negative possibility. So, using language in its normal sense, we would say that he was facing a challenge rather than a temptation. Jesus here in his prayer was not concerned with logic but with life. He bids us pray not to be delivered from challenges, but from temptations. In temptations it is evil which is endeavouring to control the situation. In challenges it is otherwise. Evil was not controlling the situation either beyond Jordan or in Gethsemane.

The third comment to be made in regard to this question merges with the third major question with which we began, which was whether there was not an absurdity in the thought that temptation was something that you had to be led into, for it was the very ground that you stood on and the air that you breathed.

Here we are driven to look at the word 'temptation', where earlier our concentration has been upon 'Lead'. Does it mean our feeling the tug of lusts and selfishness and dishonesties, or does it mean something far bigger? When we look at the New English Bible, the official and authorized translation of the New Testament for our day, which takes account of increased knowledge of the language and background of the New Testament, we find a rendering that differs quite markedly from the common one that we know and use. It runs, 'And do not bring us to the test.' Look again at that lively translation, Today's English Version, and it gives, 'Do not bring us to hard testing.' Another very recent version, the Jerusalem Bible, has, 'And do not put us to the test.'

What is the authority for this unanimity amongst recent renderings? It is that the original Greek word can mean either 'temptation' or 'test'. But this leaves us with another question. Since this alternative was there in the original word why is it that it is only in the last decade that preference has been shown for the rendering 'test'? Is it just a desire to be modern and different, and to provide greater justification for the multiplicity of modern renderings? This would scarcely account for the unanimity of choice being recently expressed. In fact it comes from a deeper study of the Lord's Prayer itself in its original setting. It is believed by many scholars that the disciples were not taught to pray to be delivered from temptation towards particular sins, but to pray not to be brought to *the* test.

What was that? For two centuries before Christ came faithful Jews had faced constant and bitter temptation to apostasize, to give up their faith under the stress and pain of persecution and perhaps the threat of death. For the first three centuries many of the followers of Christ faced the same constant temptation. Millions of our fellow-Christians have faced it in our century. They face it today.

In the light of this, the past experience of his own people and the knowledge that Jesus had of what must await his followers, is it surprising that Jesus should teach them to pray, 'Do not bring us to the test', and then add, 'But deliver us from evil'? It means then, 'If the test comes, deliver me from the great evil of apostasy, of denying the Lord I try to serve.'

How relevant a prayer that has been in our century, to Japanese Christians facing the demand to worship according to the demands of State Shintoism, to the Confessing Church in

Germany bidden trim the gospel to Nazi demands, to Kenyan Christians in the days of Mau Mau, and to Christians in many Communist-dominated territories. This is not an archaism, irrelevantly discovered by the academics; it is a petition that, understood in this way, has fitted most exactly the need of many of our fellow-Christians in our own generation.

Even those of us who do not face this kind of test from the external system of our land can still face it in our own personal experiences.

Art thou afraid his power shall fail,
When comes thine evil day?

sings Isaac Watts, from Isaiah. It is a fear that grips many of us. When grief has you by the throat, or disease begins to run down the curtain on your own life, the test comes. Humility bids us pray not to have to face the real testing that such a crunch would bring, the testing whether it has really meant anything to pray the rest of the Lord's Prayer, to call God Father, to hallow his name and yearn for his kingdom and want his will to be done.

There is something poignant in the last two-fold petition of the Lord's Prayer, 'Lead us not into temptation, but deliver us from evil.' It is a simple cry for help where it is needed most. There is something stripped and urgent about it. If we are wise, too, we shall see that it does not only need to be prayed when we are aware of the big test of faith that may lie ahead. It needs to be prayed in far more normal circumstance. 'Sometimes', says Bonhoeffer penetratingly, 'the attack (of temptation) takes the form of a false sense of security.'[6] Our betrayal of Christ may not take place when we are being severely tested in the most obvious way, by grief and suffering, but when we are letting our souls take their ease.

The cry has about it the human honesty that we ought to show in prayer. It is a form of the cry of the father who brought his epileptic son to Jesus, and was asked whether he believed. 'I have faith, help me where faith falls short.'[7] There is nothing more human in the whole of this prayer. Jesus knew that he was giving a prayer to us ordinary human beings.

NOTES

1. Marcus Dods, *Later Letters,* Hodder & Stoughton 1911, pp. 122–123.
2. Ernst Lohmeyer, *The Lord's Prayer,* Collins 1965, p. 191.
3. James 1.13 (NEB)
4. Reprinted in Joachim Jeremias, *The Prayers of Jesus,* SCM Press 1967, pp. 82–104.
5. Floyd V. Filson, *The Gospel According to St Matthew,* A & C. Black, 1960, p. 97.
6. Dietrich Bonhoeffer, *The Cost of Discipleship,* SCM Press 1948, p. 144.
7. Mark 9.24 (NEB)

10

LIBERATION FROM EVIL

The sentence 'Lead us not into temptation, but deliver us from evil' is one petition, but it contains two thoughts. The second raises such sharp issues for our praying of the Lord's Prayer today that it is worth while for our purpose to separate the two.

Once again the issue is illuminated by study of one of the words used. It is the word 'evil'. If we look at the four 'official' translations of the Bible into English we discover not only that there is a variation in translation here, but that the word used is by no means predictable by the period at which the translation was produced. All four of these translations or revisions were the result not of one scholar making his own judgment – as was the case with, say, James Moffatt or J. B. Phillips – but of groups of scholars having to find a common mind. What is interesting is that the judgment does not develop across the years; it swithers to and fro between two alternatives, the simple word 'evil' and the phrase 'the evil one'.

When the Authorized Version appeared in 1611 no one had any serious doubts of the devil's existence. It is striking therefore that the translation given there is 'evil'; the devil does not get a dishonourable mention. Then in the rather pedantic revision of 1881, just when the devil was being bowed out of sophisticated society and excluded from the minds of thoughtful men, he makes a come-back in Matthew's version of the Lord's Prayer. (Later translations than the Authorized Version delete the phrase from Luke's version of the prayer as having inadequate manuscript evidence.)

By 1946 the Authorized Version was revised again, this time by a group of American scholars, and the invaluable Revised Standard Version appeared. The devil finds no admission at this point of the gospel. Fifteen years then go by and the New English Bible appears in Britain. This is a version that is no mere revision of the past but a wholly new translation. It had its origin in an initiative within the Church of Scotland to produce a Bible that was an effective instrument for the evangelization of modern man. It is determinedly as contemporary as it can be (even if overtaken by the speed of present change in terms of 'thee' and 'thou' in addressing God by the time the full Bible appeared). Lo and behold! in this new, contemporary version for the later part of the twentieth century the devil has made a come-back. The translation is 'the evil one'.

What can account for this? The ordinary Christian may well ask, Cannot the scholars make up their minds? The difficulty is that the words used in the original Greek for 'the evil' or 'the evil one' can mean either. The noun can be masculine, meaning 'the evil one', or neuter, meaning 'evil'. In favour of judging it to be neuter, meaning evil in the abstract, there is the discovery of an Egyptian amulet of the sixth century of the Christian era in which the (slightly varied) words are clearly neuter, 'evil'. But strongly in favour of the masculine reading is the fact that of the first three gospels Matthew alone uses the phrase 'the evil one' at a number of points, whereas in the other synoptic gospels you will find names like Satan and Beelzebub which were in common use amongst the Jews at that time, or the simple description, 'the devil'.

Ernst Lohmeyer[1] draws attention to the different ways in which the first three gospel writers speak of the activity of evil in the parable of the sower. Mark has 'Satan comes', Luke 'the devil comes', but Matthew 'the evil one comes'. Moreover, the same scholar remarks that Matthew, apart from such variance in material common to the first three gospels, uses the phrase 'the evil one' particularly in sayings which appear only in that gospel, as 'Let what you say be simply "Yes" or "No"; anything more than this comes from the evil one.'[2]

This may be judged to make the personal rather than the abstract phrase more probable. No doubt it was such arguments that weighed with the translators of the New English Bible when they had to make their delicate decision. Another powerful argument would have been the increased way in which the Lord's Prayer has been seen as having to do with final things, being 'eschatalogical'. Thus, as we have seen earlier, temptation in this petition may not chiefly relate to the day-to-day plucking of evil at our sleeves, but the final test, the point at which the reality of our faith is judged. So we pray, 'Do not bring us to the test.' In the same way 'save us from the evil one' would direct our prayer towards the decisive conflict between an embattled and embodied evil and a delivering and redeeming Father.

'An embattled and embodied evil': is this more than a preacher's phrase? Today's believer may well think that if the text and honest scholarship gave the translators of our New English Bible any option it should have been firmly exercised in favour of exclusion of that *démodé* and absurd figure, a personal devil. Why put an unnecessary stumbling-block in the way of a reasonable Christian faith?

During the period when I was working on this theme I was looking in connection with other work at a book by William Temple. My eye fell on a sentence relevant to this petition which startled me. No one will doubt that Temple was possessed of a mind free from all superstition, and of singular philosophical power. But these are his words upon which my eye fell: 'Shelve the responsibility for human evil on to Satan if you will; personally I believe that he exists . . .'[3] (The rest of the quotation is not to our present purpose.) Here then is an utterly modern Christian, with one of the most powerful intelligences that

116

have graced the church of God in our century, saying calmly, and indeed in casual parenthesis, that he believes in Satan.

Now obviously we are not to take from this that Temple believed in a being with horns and a tail, complete with pitchfork for spearing recalcitrant sinners and despatching them to hell's flames. We are no more to think this than that he believed that God was a grandfatherly bearded figure ensconced on a fleecy cloud in the empyrean blue of heaven. What he meant by this otherwise startling assertion was surely that evil was personal as God is personal.

There is, of course, a problem of evil that seems impersonal. Earthquake and tidal wave, typhoon and avalanche, pose a particular problem for faith just because these apparently impersonal forces again and again most tragically engulf the lives of persons. Some forms of disease also seem to have this impersonal quality of evil (although the more we learn of the interaction of mind and spirit upon the body the less certain we can be of this). But the major problem that evil presents is in neither of these, but in the intensely personal invasion of evil into human lives which shatters our hopes, breaks our hearts and so tragically perplexes our minds.

The gain that the personification of evil in the phrase 'the evil one' brings is found just here. Many of us, with far less acute and philosophically balanced minds than William Temple's, will probably find more of an obstacle to rational faith in saying 'I believe that Satan exists' than help towards a faith relevant for this time. For us the horns and tail image, the simply incredible picture of a devilish person, may prove ineradicable in this connection. But to see evil as deeply personal may be in equal measure corrective and helpful. Seen in this way the phrase 'the evil one' reminds us of the actuality and sheer personal force of evil. Perhaps the clumsy phrase, '*the* evil', may make the point for us.

It has been well suggested that the devil never did a better day's work for himself than when he persuaded men not to believe in his existence. Once we abandoned such belief we swiftly began to find softer names for the reality that that powerful personal image had represented. So sin became maladjustment, wrong-doing, mere inadequacy in our moral education (or even just disadvantage in our environment). But calling the enemy by less fearsome names did not enable us to recruit our courage in order to fight him: on the contrary we began to persuade ourselves that he was not there, and so no conflict was demanded. His depredations upon human life and happiness became unimpeded.

All this has made some of the viler features of our century bewildering to us. We could not understand how so civilized and advanced a nation as Germany could do what was done in all its unbelievable horror to European Jewry. We are perplexed that so many of our discoveries which seem to promise much that will relieve human life of burdens and enrich human life with joys go so sour on us. They appear to add fresh and terrifying burdens, and to impoverish rather than enrich us. Of course we cannot understand, for we have denied the reality of evil.

How fascinating is the contrast between God's way with us and the way of the evil one! God *wants* us to discover his reality; he discloses himself to us. The whole story of the Bible and the whole meaning of the coming of Christ is that God makes himself known as plainly as he can. He wants us to know him, to have eyes to see his activity in the world about us, and to respond with conscious commitment to the reality of his goodness.

It is utterly different in the case of 'the evil', or 'the evil one'. Where God reveals, evil conceals. Evil wants nothing better than that we should not believe in its existence. Evil does its grimmest work on the basis of such agnosticism.

Part of the great benefit of this phrase in the Lord's Prayer is that, if we grasp its strong meaning, we take evil seriously in our prayer life. Let us pretend how we will, let us gain such false and dangerous comfort as we will, when we talk to other people, or think within ourselves, but let us face reality when we stand or kneel before God and say, 'Our Father'. Let us recognize 'the evil' – the strong, oh so strong, element in life that we rightly so designate. It is there, and reality in prayer, when illusions are stripped away, enjoins and compels that recognition

It is only when we do that that we can make the essential cry, 'Deliver us.' That cry is as important as anything in the whole prayer.

The present-day synonym for 'deliverance' that has captured our minds is 'liberation'. The ugly abbreviation 'Lib' stabs at our minds from a thousand headlines. The cry is for the liberation of women from the age-old traditions of male dominance and superiority, for the liberation of youth from the oppressive control of the older generation, for the liberation of races from exploitation and oppression. Liberation is a passion in today's world, and men and women only seek liberation if they are convinced that two things are true – that they are in bondage and that there are forces which can release them.

We have seen how subtle is the temptation to men today to deny that they are in spiritual bondage, to assert the unreality of the dark forces of evil that imprison so many human hopes. We have seen that the value even of so seemingly dated a phrase as 'the evil one' is the degree to which it forces us to recognize both the subtle personal force of evil and the power that it possesses to penetrate all that is most deeply personal in human existence.

What a glory there is in man's and woman's sexuality, and how sacramental and enhancing it can be of the fusion of two personalities at every level: but the same force can degrade men not to the level of the beasts, as is so often conventionally said, but to an acutely personal squalor of which an animal can know nothing. Again, how wonderful is the love that binds a family together, a mother's love for her children, for example. But the same love can be turned into something so different that it is no straining of language to call it diabolical. It turns thus not by changing to neglect, but by the same utterly personal force becoming demonic, a terrifying lust for possession out of which the grown children can only fight their way with a grim brutality if they are to survive as persons at all. Again, how enriching is the love of country, compounded of history, and memories and sights and sounds, and assuring familiarity, yet how often it has been degraded into supplying a strangely personal driving force for greed, brutality and tyranny.

This is our bondage from which we seek liberation, the power of 'the evil' to shadow, imprison and degrade the best things in human life. The whole Bible, in both testaments, declares God's power and purpose to effect such liberation. In the very first book of the Bible you find God given one of his most wonderful titles or descriptions, in the words set on the lips of Jacob, now known as Israel:

> The God who has led me all my life long to this day, the angel who has redeemed me from all evil.[4]

There at the beginning of the story of revelation you find God described as 'The Deliverer from Evil'; now at the close of Jesus' pattern prayer the cry is made that God will do it again for the man or company that thus cries to him.*

No part of the prayer is more an echo of Jewish prayers than this, that man should pray to his God for deliverance from evil. The best part of Jewish faith was the clarity with which they saw that the difference between good and evil was real and absolute, and that God willed good for his children. Many other contemporary faiths – even in highly developed societies like the Greek city states – did not see that the gods had anything to do with good and evil. The weakest aspect, in fact the perilous aspect, of this in our Lord's day was the degree to which the most religious elements, who were emphatic about moral distinctions,

---

* The original text of the Lord's Prayer is judged to have ended here. The doxology, 'For thine is the kingdom . . .', which follows is omitted from important manuscripts. Where it appears it varies in the words. It was probably added to form a fitting conclusion for the prayer when used in common worship.

had forgotten that evil had a power that defeated man's strongest resolution, and needed a redeeming and liberating God to give deliverance.

Again we find in a story of Jesus the most illuminating commentary on this. It is the vignette of two characters that we call the parable of the Pharisee and the publican.[5] The Pharisee is sure that firm self-discipline and well-ordered religious habit had dealt with evil for him. The publican just beats his breast and cries, 'O God, have mercy on me, sinner that I am.' It is a personal and passionate form of 'Deliver us from evil', and Jesus tells us it is that man, who so prayed, who 'went home acquitted of his sins'.

We are tempted to an almost pharisaical contempt for the Pharisee in that story, but though his self-satisfaction was gross – with perhaps an element of caricature making the point more sharply – his notion of what religion was may in fact be uncomfortably nearer to our notion of it today than we care to think. At this point the phrase 'Deliver us from evil', and our capacity to pray it with meaning and conviction, becomes a test of whether we have a living religion at all. Far too many of us, even when we have some commitment to the Christian faith, basically mistake its character at the very point which the phrase in the Lord's Prayer that we are studying illuminates. We think of faith as a set of fine and lofty moral precepts about loving God and loving our neighbour. These things are our duty and our joy, but the Christian faith is supremely a faith of deliverance. The words which were from the beginning fundamental both to it and to the Jewish faith from which it sprang are words like 'deliver', 'redeem', 'save', 'make free'. The gospel is the supreme liberation movement. It says that freedom from evil's grip is possible, and it says that God can and will give it.

'Deliver us from evil' is a cry to God in his power. It is supremely a recognition that the Father wants free sons. And, as is true right through the prayer, this petition cannot be prayed only individually. More than any other petition this one must be corporate in its whole intention, for to pray to be delivered from evil yourself, with no concern at all for the deliverance of your brother, would be to defeat your own prayer. Selfishness is one of the central forms of evil, and is not bettered but worsened by invading prayer.

Thus all the present search of men and women for liberation, when it is true human freedom in any aspect which is being sought, can be gathered up into this prayer. 'Deliver us from evil' can comprehend our prayers for mankind to know liberation from every tyranny, of past forms of sectional dominance, of racism, of political oppression, and of age-old burdens of poverty and disease.

What it must also include quite centrally is our need – and the need of all men – to know divine deliverance from 'the evil' which invades not only systems but human hearts. Many liberation movements ignore this, and the rightful desire of many Christians to align themselves with all genuine movements for human liberation may tempt them to ingore it, too. It is, but it is not only, structure and systems which oppress and imprison. Full human liberation can never be achieved by victory over external forces, but only finally by that inward deliverance which is the supreme gift of the heavenly Father to his praying children.

Right to the last phrase it is in Jesus's own life that we find the final commentary on the prayer that he taught. When he came to face the 'eschaton', the end, the final conflict with 'the evil', he prayed to be delivered. That is what happened in Gethsemane. He was delivered, not from the cup of suffering but from the power of evil. The man of faith, who prays the Lord's Prayer today, will not rightly expect to be freed from conflict with evil, or suffering at evil's hands. What he will expect with the confidence of a son is the Father's gift of freedom from evil's power. It is that liberation which enables a man to hallow God's name, to seek the coming of his kingdom, and to do his will.

NOTES

1. Ernst Lohmeyer, *The Lord's Prayer*, Collins 1965, p. 214 ff.
2. Matt. 5.37.
3. William Temple, *Nature, Man and God*, Macmillan 1934, p. 503.
4. Gen. 48.15 (AV)
5. Luke 18.10–14.